D0407760

This book belongs to

Noble's Book of
WRITING
BLUNDERS
and how to avoid them

William Noble

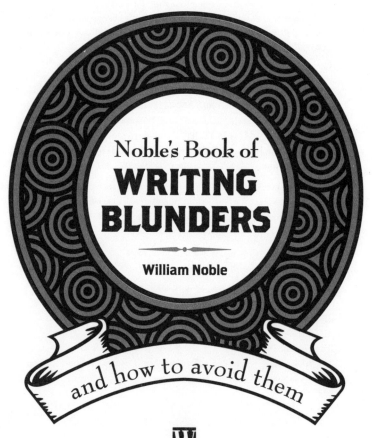

Noble's Book of
WRITING
BLUNDERS

William Noble

and how to avoid them

WRITER'S DIGEST BOOKS
Cincinnati, Ohio
www.writersdigest.com

Noble's Book of Writing Blunders and How to Avoid Them © 2006 by William Noble. Manufactured in the United States of America. All rights reserved. No part of this book may be reproduced in any form or by any electronic or mechanical means including information storage and retrieval systems without permission in writing from the publisher, except by a reviewer, who may quote brief passages in a review. Published by Writer's Digest Books, an imprint of F+W Publications, Inc., 4700 East Galbraith Road, Cincinnati, Ohio, 45236. (800) 289-0963. First edition.

11 10 09 08 07   5 4 3 2 1

Distributed in Canada by Fraser Direct, 100 Armstrong Avenue, Georgetown, ON, Canada L7G 5S4, Tel: (905) 877-4411. Distributed in the U.K. and Europe by David & Charles, Brunel House, Newton Abbot, Devon, TQ12 4PU, England, Tel: (+44) 1626 323200, Fax: (+44) 1626 323319, E-mail: pos tmaster@davidandcharles.co.uk. Distributed in Australia by Capricorn Link, P.O. Box 704, Windsor, NSW 2756 Australia, Tel: (02) 4577-3555.

Visit our Web site at www.writersdigest.com for information on more resources for writers. To receive a free weekly e-mail newsletter delivering tips and updates about writing and about Writer's Digest products, register directly at our Web site at http://newsletters.fwpublications.com.

Library of Congress Cataloging-in-Publication Data

Noble, William.
  Noble's book of writing blunders / William Noble. -- 1st ed.
      p. cm.
  Includes index.
  ISBN-13: 978-1-58297-475-0 (hardcover : alk. paper)
  ISBN-10: 1-58297-475-6
  1. English language--Style. 2. English language--Rhetoric. 3. Style, Literary.
  4. English language--Grammar. I. Title.
  PE1421N63 2007
  808'.042--dc22   2006023152

Edited by Amy Schell
Designed by Grace Ring
Production coordinated by Mark Griffin

Dedication

For John, Leslie, and Nataleigh

About the Author

William Noble is the author or co-author of twenty books and several hundred shorter works in a writing career spanning more than thirty-five years. His books for writers, each of which was a main selection of the Writer's Digest Book Club, include: *Steal This Plot*, *"Shut Up!" He Explained*, *Show Don't Tell*, *Make That Scene*, and *Writing Dramatic Nonfiction*. His *Conflict, Action & Suspense* is part of Writer's Digest's Elements of Fiction Writing series, and his *BookBanning In America* was nominated for the Eli Oboler Award of the American Library Association's Intellectual Freedom Roundtable.

Prior to writing full time, he practiced law in Pennsylvania, having earned his J.D. from the University of Pennsylvania and his B.A. from Lehigh University. Currently, he writes the "Gourmet Golf" column in and is a contributing editor for the golf magazines of Divot Communication. He teaches creative writing at Georgian Court University in Lakewood, New Jersey and online with the Community College of Vermont.

He lives along the New Jersey shore in a quiet village without on-street mail delivery, and he can be reached at wllmnob@aol.com.

TABLE OF CONTENTS

INTRODUCTION

When I spoke with the editors at Writer's Digest about this book, they were clear on what they wanted: "Concentrate on style, on uniqueness of the author's presentation," they suggested. "Writers shouldn't assume a literal approach, they should treat ... well, grammar, for instance, more broadly, more flexibly."

"This isn't a book about grammar," I reminded them.

"But it's about style and attitude, and grammar can't be ignored."

Style and attitude have been the beacons of my attention, but grammar approach and usage are part of the circle of light. This book is about style and flair and the writing of good prose; it shows grammar technique and attitude as "tools," not as ends in themselves. I'd like to think I've urged a way of thinking, not a rote application of iron-fast rules about punctuation and syntax. Be flexible, I've wanted to say. Think imaginatively.

And avoid those big writing blunders that can squeeze the life out of what you write. For instance, if all of us followed the same grammar rules and thought in the same grammar terms, there would be little distinction in our styles, in the *way* we write. One piece of writing would read and sound like every other piece of writing, and instead of individuality, there would be only a collective *us*!

Fortunately, the demands of style and individuality allow you to avoid the straightjacket of rules and formulas. It comes back to attitude, of course, where you become what you think you are,

and if you strive to develop an *individual* voice because you're willing to be more flexible and imaginative, then that's what will eventually appear. Adhering to all the rules—grammar and otherwise—will prevent you from exerting your individuality because you'll certainly sound like everyone else. But attitude is more than seeking to break rules simply because they are there; you must have a reason beyond the urge to be different. There must be *purpose* in what you do. Your style must benefit, and so must the reader's sense of enjoyment.

A running presence through this book will be my conviction that readers not only read words on a page but "hear" them as well. That is, as the reader's eyes fall on the words her ears will pick up the sound of the words, too. Some call it the "music" of words, and it can't be overlooked when you're working on style. One way of understanding the influence of rules—grammar or otherwise—on the way you write is to see how they affect the word sounds. Will italics, generally used for emphasis, also change the point of view, for example, and if so, how effectively? Does capitalizing an entire phrase and running the words together cause the words to scream out at the reader? Questions like these are what the thinking writer must pose to herself, and the answers will determine whether the word sounds are sour or sweet.

Attitude is what you're after, remember. Style is what you hope to produce.

Flexibility and imagination are the keys, and the door to better writing can be opened ...

If you're ready to turn the handle.

1

DON'T WRITE FOR YOUR EIGHTH-GRADE TEACHER

"There are certain writing rules we have to learn," said the stern-faced woman who was my eighth-grade teacher. She was tall and angular, darkish hair pulled to a modified bun and sharp eyes that missed little. It was the beginning of the school year, and most of us still remembered with fondness the urgings of our seventh-grade teacher: "Use your *minds*, young people; show your imaginations. I want ideas, I want good stories."

The eighth-grade teacher loomed over us now, rolling a piece of chalk in her fingers. As she spoke, the image of that agreeable seventh-grade experience faded. It was obvious that things would be different, and none of us was certain if we were going to like it. Eighth grade, we knew, was a big step, and we'd heard this teacher could make the entire year seem like a century if she chose to.

We waited, our collective confidence on a knife edge.

She walked to the board and wrote out a declarative sentence. "What word is the subject?" she asked.

We told her.

"And the predicate?"

"The verb, you mean?" My best friend volunteered that.

She turned, her glare icy. "I *mean* the predicate."

We told her, and she began to draw a series of lines and boxes around, over, and under the words in the sentence. Then she put the chalk down and smiled at us. "This is the way you diagram a

Noble's Blunders
4

sentence," she said. "When we're finished, you'll be able to see it like the pieces of a jigsaw puzzle, and you'll understand the rules of proper grammar."

And for the balance of that school year we did, indeed, learn that there were grammar rules, and we saw how they were applied in such books as *The Adventures of Huckleberry Finn*, *A Tale of Two Cities* and *The Good Earth*. We used the rules in our own writing, and we came to understand quickly that grammar rules improperly applied brought the wrath of our teacher and a lower grade.

"There are certain writing rules we *have* to learn," she said, and she was absolutely correct ... as long as we were in the eighth grade. That was the time to learn how to diagram a sentence, where to place commas, when to use a participial phrase, whether to place the adjective in front of or after the noun it modifies. These grammar rules (and many more, as well) were necessary to learn so that we could develop order in our writing and understand the rules' purposes. What she didn't tell us, but what we also came to understand, was that once we knew the rules, we could feel comfortable violating them.

Because the grammar rules we learned in eighth grade should never be followed absolutely. At best, they are one choice among several, and at worst, they will dampen our creative instincts.

Take a look at what I've just written. I used "because" to begin the sentence. My eighth-grade teacher would be horrified. "Never *ever* use a conjunction to begin a sentence!" But read it again. Doesn't it flow smoothly from the immediately preceding paragraph? It connects the two paragraphs easily and simply, yet it's a different enough thought and subject that it should exist in its own paragraph.

Why the rule about conjunctions, then? Probably because anything labeled a conjunction means that it must join two parallel, roughly similar sentences, and if it begins a sentence, how can it join them within the same sentence? It may also be that eighth-

grade grammar teachers like their prose clean and declarative with the subject matter modified or reduced.

But good writing isn't so sanitized. Look to the master of the declarative sentence, Ernest Hemingway. In the space of four pages in "The Snows of Kilimanjaro" he writes:

"And just then it occurred to him he was going to die."

"But the lovers bored her."

"But perhaps he wouldn't."

Each one of these is a separate sentence and a conjunction begins them. "And" and "but" are the most usual conjunctions, and my eighth-grade teacher would not have stood still for my using them to start a sentence. But as a writer, you have to understand that when a sentence calls for a conjunction to start it off, that's the way it should be, rule or no rule. What you're seeking is a rhythm of sorts, where the word-flow continues smoothly, and for that you have to recognize that the reader not only "hears" what she reads, but sees the words, too. A longish sentence with a conjunction between two or more parallel thoughts might slow down the prose while two separate sentences might speed it up. The most important thing is to keep the reader's interest, and breaking up a lengthy sentence into snappier portions (which could include a conjunction to lead off) might work better.

And if you'll look up the page, you'll notice I have started off two sentences, including one paragraph, with "But" ... and this paragraph and sentence with "And."

How about this rule? *You can't split an infinitive!* Seems reasonable, doesn't it? "To *sometimes* go ..." "To *possibly* solve ..." "To *suddenly* swim ..." are a bit disjointed; wouldn't it read better to put the intruding adverb before or after the infinitive? An infinitive phrase, by its nature, is in two parts, and grammarians must have felt unsettled to see that tandem broken. Inserting a splitter can

have the effect of reducing the impact of the infinitive. Wouldn't it be better if you produce "to write disjointedly" instead of "to disjointedly write?"

Yet, the trend these days has been toward decoupling the parts of the infinitive. The reason seems to be that the purist writing we learned back in eighth grade has traces of Victorian formality; since the 1960s, there has been a movement toward more colloquial writing, and one indication of this is the splitting of infinitives. How often do you hear it in conversation now? People split infinitives more or less readily, and if it's in conversation, it will be on the page eventually. And sometimes it reads better, too. Is there a better way of writing, "No one knows how to really handle this?" Try to move it around and keep the infinitive unsplit. It really can't be done.

Nor should it really be tried.

Remember this rule? *You will not end a sentence with a preposition!* The reason's clear enough: a preposition's purpose is to introduce something else, not to end it. A sentence ending with a preposition has a tendency to leave things dangling, unfinished, as if the story has come to the edge of a cliff and there's no support left. A reader could feel dissatisfied and misused.

My eighth-grade teacher would rephrase, "Where did you jump off from?" as "From where did you jump?" Obviously better English and classically correct. It even carries smoother rhythm; there's nothing awkward in the sounds or the meaning.

But if a character has an eighth-grade education (and was never exposed to my eighth-grade teacher) the chances are he'd be less scrupulous about the rules of grammar and might easily end sentences with prepositions (to say nothing about double negatives or mismatched subjects and predicates). The point is there is a time to ignore the rules of grammar, and this is certainly one of them. If you have your characters always speaking and responding in perfect, correct English, you're going to bore the reader who is

actually looking for something in the characters to identify with. Readers understand what correct language is, but readers also understand that no one speaks perfectly all the time!

And did you notice I ended a sentence with a preposition two sentences back? Did it seem awkward or misplaced? Only a bit more colloquial, perhaps, and what's wrong with that? As a writer, you want people to read your material, and the more formally you present it (that is, the closer you adhere to the *proper* grammar rules) the cooler your writing becomes. When that happens, you're going to lose some audience because readers by and large wish to be entertained. That's best done with more colloquial language.

Not always, of course. "Whom did you take the measure of?" is awkward phrasing. It's jerky and dangling. Isn't it smoother to write, "Whose measure did you take?"

How about: "The road went through the trees to the barn, which it circled outside of"? Here again is some awkward phrasing, mainly because of the ending preposition. See how much smoother it becomes: "The road went through the trees and circled outside of the barn."

Yet there are many times when a sentence-ending preposition is the best choice. Joseph Conrad talked about "the heart within," and this was the way he would end things. Colloquialisms have sprung up, too: "What's he all about?" ... "He's on the inside!" ... It's impossible to insist on a proper grammar rule when our language has carved so many exceptions. What's better is to acknowledge that the colloquialism or grammar exception should be used and then sense the word-flow. Is it smooth enough? Does it fit with the story?

Not a complete sentence!

Remember this criticism? No verb, perhaps, or only the fragment of a thought. Our eighth-grade teacher saw this as a deadly challenge to the foundations of written English. ("Sentences are

meant to have subjects and predicates, *at least!*") Here again the rule made sense because most sentences have subjects and verbs, and we were learning about other people's expectations.

But incomplete sentences work, too. So do sentence fragments. It depends upon emphasis and rhythm. A single word repeated over and over, for example:

Yes, yes, yes ... !

Or phrase:

How now, brown cow?

No subjects or verbs here, yet you get a message across to the reader. There's an abruptness with incomplete sentences or sentence fragments precisely because they don't follow the conventional structure. They can force a change of pace.

Don't overdo it, though. Too much of anything destroys the effect, so the usual sentence (subject, verb plus objects) should remain the customary approach.

With a nod toward the exceptions—sentence fragments and incomplete sentences.

There's one thing to remember about the rules of grammar, as you shall see throughout this book. They are not rigid; they change as our perceptions of our language change. What satisfied our eighth-grade teacher certainly wouldn't satisfy an editor, but then our eighth-grade teacher wasn't trying to be an editor. The rules, however, were there to be learned, and once we learned them, we could believe they applied only when they made our work better.

Samuel Johnson said it well: "The pen must at length comply with the tongue." If our colloquialisms come to violate the rules of grammar, as we learned them in eighth grade, the chances are the rules of grammar will change.

And the writer who understands this is the writer who's taken a creative step up ...

(See, I ended with a preposition.)

Blunder No. 1

DON'T COMPLICATE
THE OBVIOUS

Sooner or later, anyone who has taken a writing class comes up against the criticism, "You're using a cliché! Writers are supposed to be creative." There's not a writer among us who hasn't faced this stylistic dragon and come away unsettled. The truth is that the creative mind doesn't always burst with innovation; there are times when you find yourself thinking along well-trodden paths *and not realizing it!*

Clichés are, after all, words and phrases that have become overused because they support timelessly the theme or situation they describe. You hear them or read them so often they affix themselves to your subconscious like microorganisms, and their infection can spread. What you strive for is the ability to avoid them completely, but we all know that's impossible. The next best thing is to recognize them when you are tempted to use them and to come up with something else.

The problem so many writers have is that sometimes the cure can be worse than the disease. In our zeal to be truly innovative, we produce something that would leave hapless readers—well, hapless. Our creative minds conjure a word or phrase or grammar technique that might satisfy the gods of innovation, but few readers would be able to tag along. (How about consecutive pages of all-caps, followed by consecutive pages of no-caps and no punctuation either!) We take a perfectly simple situation and proceed to complicate it, striving to blunt criticism of our writing.

We work so hard searching for the "creative" solution that we neglect the obvious usefulness of what we already have. Simply put: There are certain writing mechanisms that should *not* be fiddled with. The period at the end of the sentence, for instance. It seems simplistic to even mention it—everyone *knows* sentences end with a period.

Yet, the inexperienced writer might convince himself that even the period should go in favor of some other mark, or perhaps no mark at all.

What if all the book's sentences were to end with semicolons;
Or dashes--
Or an upside down exclamation point¡
Or nothing

At a minimum things would be confusing, and it's not hard to imagine a descent into chaos. But that's all right, says the inexperienced writer. I'm trying to do something *different*. I'm creative!

Silly would be more like it. The period at the end of a sentence serves a useful and necessary purpose. It informs the reader that a certain action or thought has paused (think of a speaker who must take periodic breaths) and it allows the writer to string his work in sections, thus providing necessary rhythm and cadence.

This isn't to say a period can never be omitted; only that doing it for the purpose of innovation is dangerous and usually unsuccessful. In the right hands, though, it can work well. Take *Ulysses* by James Joyce. In the last chapter, he begins:

> Yes because he never did a thing like that before to ask to get his breakfast in bed with a couple of eggs since the *City Arms* hotel when he used to be pretending to be laid up with a sick voice doing his highness to made himself interesting to that old faggot Mrs. Riordan that he thought he had a great leg of and she never left us a farthing all for masses for herself and her soul greatest miser ever was actually afraid to lay out 4d for her methylated spirit telling me all her ailments she had too much old chat in her about politics and earthquakes and the end of the world...

He continues for about forty pages in this stream of consciousness, thousands of words flowing across the page, none separated by a period. Certainly it's innovative; yet, it works because Joyce is portraying the jumbled thoughts and ideas that spark through our minds as we think, and our minds do not work in sentences with periods. Joyce was not doing this solely to be innovative; he had a clear purpose, and generations have applauded him for it.

And he was not so taken with a lack of periods that he followed this style throughout the book. In fact, most of the book has conventional sentences that end in periods, and that should tell us something; even the most innovative style is grounded in immutable, uncomplicated techniques most of the time.

But the writer's imagination really knows no bounds when it comes to seeking something different, and if you push yourself far enough, the chances are what's different is to have complicated an essentially straightforward situation. Openings, closing, scene changes, chapter arrangements ... all of these are pure and basic structure for stories. The writer who manipulates these in the name of innovation is sadly misguided. An opening that places the reader in the middle of the action serves to develop and propel the writer-reader partnership, and anything that disturbs it—especially in the name of innovation—could mortally wound the story.

Suppose, for example, the opening three paragraphs of your story are nothing but a series of misspelled words. Without an explanation, the reader would certainly be confused, and even with the explanation, the story's dramatic effect could be lost. You may be beaming because the writing was certainly innovative, but for what purpose? The story opening has been nullified, and the reader's attention has most likely been lost.

Or take closings. There's a logical place to stop a story, to end it, and the way it's done is similar to placing the cap back on the bottle after we've refreshed ourselves. Either you connect back to the story beginning or you play the circumstances out until the

certainties you've created have been resolved. Either way, ending a story is a simple process, relatively speaking, once you feel you've satisfied the reader. The more complicated you make it, the more risk you take that the reader will go away unsatisfied.

Suppose you end your story with a series of symbolic grammar marks that might mean something to you, but have no relevance to the reader? Your purpose may be innovation, but who's to know? All you've succeeded in doing is to confuse the reader and to leave him with distinct dissatisfaction. Should you decide to explain what the symbolic grammar marks mean, you end up telling the reader instead of showing and, as we all know, this does away with dramatic effect. In your creative mind these symbolic grammar marks (or other complicating devices) might stand for something wise and profound, a proper ending to the story, but chances are the reader won't catch it.

The same could be said for chapter arrangements and scene changes. There are good reasons for these devices, and a writer who monkeys around with them had better have strong purpose to fulfill. It isn't enough to want to be different; that's like wearing a gorilla suit to a wedding—different, yes, but hardly appropriate. Dividing a book into chapters and scenes gives the reader (and writer) a chance to pause, to take stock, and perhaps to change direction. (One obvious technique is permitting a change in point of view.) It permits the development of subplots and additional characterizations; it allows the writer to maintain a tight hold on the story and not lose control. In fact, it is an expression of our own humanness because we tend to look at life—ours as well as others—in chapters and scenes. Marriages or schooling or friendships or individual jobs (the list can be endless) are self-limiting experiences in the sense that we can trace them from their beginnings, and we can focus on them. We've all heard people speak of certain experiences as "that chapter of my life" or "I was happy to get out of that scene," and we know exactly what they mean.

So, too, with writing. Books have chapters and scenes because they are read most easily that way. We are familiar with the approach, and we know it works well. Any writer who seeks to change that (for example, running an unbroken narrative from page one to the end of the book without paragraphing or without chapters; leaving three-quarters of a page blank between scenes) must recognize the jolt this will give readers. A book divided into chapters and scenes allows thought processes to regroup periodically and to stop the story at convenient places, while assuring readers they will be missing nothing if they put the book down for a little while.

Imagine the reader who has no guide like this. Confusion, perhaps even anger, could result. Robert Frost, opining about free verse, wrote of "playing tennis without a net." This is the same thing … unless there's a strong reason. Readers need guideposts, and chapters and scenes provide these.

It's possible, of course, to succeed without chapters and scenes (stream-of-consciousness writing is one clear example), but the writers who mastered the technique are on a short list indeed: Virginia Woolf, Marcel Proust, William Faulkner, among others. They were able to get away with it because they had purpose in what they did. There was a reason for complicating the obvious, and this made it exciting literature instead of only being "different."

DON'T BE A SLAVE TO A GRAMMAR GURU

How many times have you heard, "Start by writing one simple declarative sentence"? It's universal advice, and its origins are probably buried in journalistic lore where the premium has been on presenting unvarnished prose. At some point, fiction writers came to see the advice as good for them, too, and so the idea of writing one simple declarative sentence became more than a writing approach—it became a writing style. Writers not only thought in declarative sentences, they wrote them, again and again. Inevitably, a writer would emerge who would turn the declarative sentence into an art form, and thus, the style and concepts of a generation of writers would reflect this influence.

That writer was Ernest Hemingway, and when he wrote, "The day had been hot. I had been up the river to the bridgehead at Plava. It had been there that the offensive was to begin ..." (*A Farewell to Arms*), others started to imagine they could write that way, too. It isn't difficult to write a simple declarative sentence:

"The rifle was long and cold and strange ..."

"She wore black shoes, a red cape, and a white tunic ..."

"The beast snuffled in agony on the blood-soaked sand ..."

The art comes in stringing these sentences together and then adding dialogue and narrative description that sparks the reader's imagination and creates magnificent images. Few could do that

well, but many tried. With multitudes aping his style, Hemingway became a grammar guru. People tried to write short, snappy sentences, declarative statements that hit the reader between the eyes. It meant using active verbs only, avoiding compound sentences, and using single-syllable adjectives.

The problem was that as more and more writers adopted his style and grammar, Hemingway's prose techniques lost their freshness and, in time, became vulnerable to parody. Then the writers who thought they had a good thing when they began to write like Hemingway found there was no room in the market for Hemingway look-alikes when the real Hemingway was still around, and he could write this way better than anyone else.

These Hemingway stylists did themselves a disservice as well. By devoting time and energy to writing like someone else, they neglected their own development, and when they finally broke away, they could only founder.

This doesn't mean that the simple declarative sentence should not be used. It's a staple for many writers and writing styles for good reason. It is the clearest form of expression, and all forms of writing need that. Most savvy writers avoid trying to write *exactly* the way Hemingway did and just use his sentence structure, his verb voices, and his adjective limitations.

Don't be a slave to Hemingway, but use him to develop a personal approach: perhaps declarative sentences at key places but not in machine gun order; or fewer, more fulsome adjectives; or more dialogue and less description.

The point is: Make grammar and style innovations from your own creative pot; cook up your own mix.

It's important to understand why certain grammar and style techniques work because that will give you a handle on what you might try in your own work. Take Kurt Vonnegut, for example. In several of his books, he uses the phrase "and so it goes ..." to end a scene or a chapter. What's it mean? Why does he use it?

His purpose is to denote the banality of horrific events such as the Allied fire bombing of the city of Dresden during World War II. Thousands upon thousands were incinerated, homes and factories and offices and museums were destroyed, all in the name of winning the war. In his novel *Slaughterhouse-Five*, he describes the destruction and killing, and from time to time he ends a scene or a chapter with "… and so it goes …" which might also have said "So what else is new?" The war itself was replete with horrifying events such as this, so why get more worked up here? Horror was an everyday circumstance.

His little ending phrase, then, merely underscores his thesis. It adds his own voice to the circumstances, so the reader knows exactly how he feels, too. Kurt Vonnegut, instead of inserting an exclamation point where the horrific events are rolled out or using italics to highlight the terror, adds a simple phrase and accomplishes the same purpose.

And it's fresh, it's innovative.

But that doesn't mean we should use it, too. Vonnegut developed his thesis over the course of an entire book, and he used the phrase at appropriate times to buttress what he was trying to get across. It was effective because it fit the novel he wrote, and clearly it might not fit where the thesis of banality (it needn't be horror, it could be greed or self-absorption, for example) was not present.

"… And so it goes …" is a stylistic and grammatical triumph because it dovetailed with the entire story. Used any other way it would be awkward and clumsy and certainly inappropriate.

And that's why you shouldn't be so quick to borrow things like this. If a well-known writer developed certain innovative grammar and style forms, there was a purpose behind the creation of those forms. The writer worked them out to give added substance to his or her prose. If you lift them completely and insert them in *your* prose, the fit may be wasted because your purpose isn't the same.

Take James Joyce again. In *Ulysses* he developed the stream-of-consciousness technique where punctuation marks were almost non-existent when he was in his character's head. Sometimes sentences ran on for pages, and his idea of grammar was to use it sparingly, if at all, when the stream of consciousness was in effect. Sentences banged together without capitals and periods, phrases would dangle, and sometimes, whole words would lose their final syllables. But there was a purpose here. Our minds don't work in final drafts, so jumbled thoughts and ideas, unfinished and unsettled, are realistic.

With *Ulysses*, James Joyce certainly became a grammar guru. But following *his* stream-of-consciousness techniques slavishly will probably bring a flood of rejection slips. His entire story took place over a twenty-four hour period, so he could concentrate his character insights in stream of consciousness because the plot line was almost subordinate to who the characters were. Few people write like this, and it requires great skill to produce lengthy, ungrammatical narrative that can be understood and embraced. After all, it took Joyce seven years to write *Ulysses*, and the grammar techniques he used had to be carefully fitted with the prose. Could we expect the same kind of fit with our prose?

But that doesn't mean you can't profit from understanding Joyce or Vonnegut or any other grammar guru. Instead of using "and so it goes …" come up with something of your own. The idea of placing a small half-phrase at the end of chapters or scenes that sums up the underlying thesis is a good one. All you need to do is come up with your own word or phrase.

Even your own punctuation mark. Tom Wolfe, in much of his writing, allows sentences to dangle with ellipsis points (…), providing not a pause but a sense that things will go on and on, the same way, without deviation. He offers punctuation because it's different and because those overly familiar words—"and things were about to change" or "he could sense things never changing" — wouldn't grace the page.

You can do the same thing, but where Tom Wolfe uses ellipses throughout his work, be more judicious. Tom Wolfe has a certain style—jaunty, disdainful—and his ellipses give it effect by showing that nothing should be taken too seriously, that whatever the situation, it will go on and on. Unless you duplicate Tom Wolfe's style, you shouldn't use ellipsis points the way he does, and when you do use them, consider whether they might not stand for another purpose altogether (such as a pause). For ellipsis points (or any other specialized punctuation mark), the tie-in with the style and the purpose of what you're writing must be made.

By all means learn from the grammar gurus. See how they utilize their innovative techniques; understand what they are trying to do.

But then apply your own learning by dabbing it on your own work. Don't try to copy the techniques completely—try to fit their purposes with yours. You benefit two ways: You get to use innovative techniques, and you're bound to find some added zest in your style.

DON'T LET THAT
POINT OF VIEW WAVER

The storyline is simple: a young man and his fiancée are attending a museum opening …

> He had never been a museumgoer, he acknowledged to himself, and he recalled with an inward chuckle how his mother despaired of his cultural awareness.
>
> "How do you expect to learn about things," she would complain.
>
> He'd shrug and change the subject …

As this story unfolds, it's clear the young man's perspective is driving the storyline. We're in his head, we're seeing the developing story as he sees it, we're feeling what he's feeling … whether it's wonder at the frequency that evenings like this will occur in his upcoming marriage, or the acknowledgment that he was never a museumgoer, or the further recollection of his mother's despair and his reaction to it.

What we're seeing is the portrayal of point of view; that is, we're reading the story, at least in this initial stage, from the young man's perspective. Everything he sees, touches, feels, smells, and tastes is fair game to explore because we're inside his head and his body, and it's his point of view through which the story unfolds.

To many, "point of view" seems a disarmingly simple concept: tell the story through one character's eye and all will be revealed.

Simple, perhaps, but much more difficult to execute.

What happens if the writer wants to include another character's internal reaction in the same scene? Suppose the story jumps to the fiancée's point of view:

> She knew he'd rather be watching the ballgame tonight, and she felt pleasurable warmth at his willingness to do what she wanted to do; he's a good man, she told herself, he'll make a fine husband ...

Or what happens if the writer wishes to intrude himself into the storyline?

> Unconsciously, he removed his hand from the wheel, rubbing his chin in that studied way he had ...

What's occurring here is a switch in point of view. In effect, the spotlight of attention, however briefly, moves somewhere else, and the reader is forced to shift her involvement in the story. In the first example, we've shifted it to the woman's perspective as she contemplates his willingness to do what she wanted him to do, and we even explore her internal measure of him as a man. But note that as we do this, we drop our involvement with the man in order to pick up involvement with the woman. In the process, we've lost something: a sense of identity with a character – the man – with whom we opened the scene. Now, we have to gather ourselves and try to identify with the woman, a more difficult task because we're really beginning all over again in the middle of the scene.

In the second example, we've shifted, not to the woman, but to the author who tells us the man has "unconsciously" removed his hand from the wheel and is "rubbing" his chin in a "studied way." Note how the author intrudes here: it's as if he is standing by, as a witness, describing for us the man's unconscious action of removing his hand and rubbing his chin. But if we had remained with the man's point of view, his "unconscious" movement would not have been possible since he wouldn't have been aware of it; the only one who could inform us about it is the author himself.

Hence, the point of view has shifted to the author. Note, also, that the rub of the chin is modified by "unconsciously" so the character does this in the same way he removes his hand from the wheel. It is the author who is providing this perspective, not the character, and thus, the point of view is shifted.

What happens is that once the author intrudes, the character's point of view is lost, even if temporarily, and the reader sees things from a more remote perspective. That's because the author's intrusion resembles the arrival of a witness who sees and concludes in ways different from how the character might see and conclude. Before the intrusion, the character is a participant, more closely involved in the storyline than the witness-author.

The effect, then, is to push reader involvement back a step, which could have the consequence of impeding reader identification with the character.

The late editor William Sloane referred to point of view as "means of perception," as in, through whose "means of perception" does the author wish the scene to proceed? Whose perspective, whose "eye" will control the unfolding storyline? For Sloane, author intrusion, as above, was akin to receiving a phone call from an unfamiliar voice, which fails to identify itself. It interrupts, it interferes, it intrudes.

And it also shifts the point of view or means of perception. "More fiction fails because the author has not had the discipline and ingenuity to provide and sustain a means of perception than for any other single reason," Sloane wrote in *The Craft of Writing*, and this is especially true when it comes to author intrusion. Remove, he advised, "every paragraph, every sentence, every word where the author has briefed the reader—told him rather than shown him something the author wants him to know so that he can get on with the story ..."

A skillful writer will recognize that solid point of view is dependent upon a simple—though major—decision at the outset:

who speaks! Whose means of perception will control story progress, whose eye will focus on characters, setting and plot, whose point of view will be dominant? Novelist Janet Burroway calls this the "primary" step the writer must take to focus on the story.

Who speaks? In what form? First person, third person, even second person (though quite rare)? Through which character will the means of perception be portrayed, and will it be depicted in first person or third person?

Obvious, isn't it? Deciding *who speaks!* is not simple, but it is necessary for the storyline to hold together. Inevitably, some writers push the envelope and seek to add a plural response to *who speaks!* That is, they shift the scene perspective so *who speaks!* moves and the means of perception changes from one character to another.

If this is done on a chapter-by-chapter basis or even on a scene-by-scene basis, few readers would complain (see, for example, William Faulkner's *As I Lay Dying* which has a different character's point of view with each chapter.) The natural break between chapters or between scenes sets the stage for the change and clues the reader into it.

Problems develop, however, when the shift takes place *within* the scene. There are accomplished writers who can make it work (such as Alice Adams in her story "The Party-Givers"), but to do so requires not only total control of language and detail but also portrayal which provides something from each character's point of view that could not be learned from any other character's point of view. Pulling this off can be a daunting task. In effect, it requires the writer to run parallel races on parallel tracks, shifting the perspective from runner to runner as the race proceeds.

A difficult undertaking, especially within the confines of a single scene. For William Sloane, the question of avoiding point-of-view switch really goes to the heart of the fiction-writing process. "Anything a writer does that deepens reader involvement

strengthens the fiction," he felt, adding that the experience of reading fiction through one of the characters is "all-absorbing." And it goes without saying that the more a reader learns about a character, the more that reader's involvement and interest in the story will deepen. Sloane puts it simply: "There is in successful fiction one and only one means of perception to a scene."

The tendency, especially among less experienced writers, is to shift the point of view within a scene in order to portray as much as possible (the thinking: if some is good, why wouldn't more be better?). But this defeats the very purpose of gaining reader involvement, which is what every writer strives for. The deeper that involvement, the more affected the reader will be, and the more affected the reader will be, the greater the respect for the writer.

William Sloane insisted there should be only one "means of perception" to a scene.

Don't let it waver; don't let it shift!

DON'T FREEZE AND FORMALIZE LANGUAGE

It happens each year in my writing classes—always with the first or second writing assignment. After I have carefully explained that the process of writing includes reading aloud to a group of one's peers and gaining feedback in the form of constructive criticism, there are worried faces.

"You'll see," I tell them. "It'll help."

Few believe me, of course.

At the next class, where some readings will take place, one student will be sitting ramrod straight, face frozen. "I don't want to read," this student will say.

"Why?" I know the answer, of course.

He nods at his manuscript. "It's too personal." Then he adds: "I'd let you see it, though."

"You feel vulnerable, that it?"

"It's personal stuff."

I explain that all writing is "personal stuff"; there isn't one of us who doesn't project some of himself into everything he writes. We write for readers, not for *a* reader, and the purpose of art is to divulge our point of view in dramatic form. If you squeeze out the so-called personal stuff, you are left with stiff, formal material that divides you from your readers. Instead of projecting warmth and getting involved with your readers, you turn cold.

Obviously, there are situations where coldly formal writing is appropriate. In court, for example, you wouldn't expect a lawyer's brief

to be structured like a novel with dialogue and characterization and plot development. And in academia, the analytic treatise is hardly a bedtime story. The purpose in either case is to appeal to the intellect, not establish emotional involvement, and cold formality works well.

But with fiction or dramatic nonfiction, you need to involve the reader through an emotional tie, and the warmer you make your prose, the easier the tie will be to establish. By warmer, I mean less formal, less standoffish. (I don't mean "practice writing" or "writing exercise.") You must warm up your writing if you expect the reader to get into the story, and the way to do it is to make the writing more easily understood and more personal.

Grammar plays a big part in all of this because it provides techniques for helping the warm-up. An occasional word here or there, a punctuation mark changed or removed, a shift in person or point of view, and the warm-up has progressed. But it can't work well unless solid, meaningful words are used.

Which is warmer and more personal?

Despite the fact the sun was so uncomfortable, I kept my sweater on ...

Yet the broiling sun didn't force me to pull off my sweater ...

The second line, obviously. There's formality in the first line, where the second is more colloquial, and, hence, warmer.

Simple as it sounds, one of the ways we can warm up our prose is to use contractions, make our phrasing more colloquial. Experienced writers know that softening words will have them land more gently on the reader's ear because a reader "hears" as well as sees what you write. He follows the prose rhythms and absorbs the sounds of the words, and when the sounds are softer, they are more agreeable. Note how differently the following sentence sounds without and with contractions:

It is not that I would rather you go, but Jim is not experienced; he does not understand you do not barge in on the Judge ...

> It's not I'd rather you go, but Jim isn't so experienced; he doesn't under-
> stand you don't barge in on the Judge ...

Read them both aloud and watch the formality drain away with
the second version. The words are brought closer to the reader
and made more personal because they've become colloquial. We
hear and speak contractions most of the time, so it's natural to
use them in your writing, especially if you want to bridge identity with readers.

There are times when you don't want to use contractions because you want to keep your writing formal. That's true with certain types of exposition where you explain or define, but it's also
true with characterization. Sometimes you may wish a character to
speak without contractions, and in this way paint him as coldly formal (such as where the character might be reading a speech, and
you wish to stress the dignity of the situation). It wouldn't make
the character more likeable, but that may be precisely your point.
Avoid the contractions and ice up the mood ... and the characters.

Suppose you want to change the mood of a sentence or a page.
Suppose, for example, you write: *My mother and sister warned me
about the cave* ... and you want to get across the idea that in spite of
the warning, you decided to explore the cave? The phase already
written carries the idea of danger and uncertainty, and now you're
faced with what William Zinsser calls "mood changers"—that
is, key words that can be inserted to signal the change of mood
in the sentence. *You* know you're going to change the sentence
mood, but the reader does not, and so without some signal from
you that the sentence mood will be changing, the reader could
end up confused. Suppose the sentence read:

> My mother and sister warned me about the cave, and I decided to
> explore it ...

We have a possible mood change—from danger and uncertainty to bravado and certainty. Yet, we have no signal for mood

change, so the reader may assume that danger and uncertainty prevails when actually you wanted to get across that bravado and certainty are the newest feelings. But there's nothing to distinguish the two moods, nothing to break them up and show they are different. If you fail to project *this*, you end up distancing yourself from your readers.

There are key words that can be used as mood changers, and these do two things: They signal the mood change (and thereby alert the reader), and they smooth out your writing. See how much clearer the sentence reads:

> My mother and sister warned me about the cave, *but* I decided to explore it ...

Exchanging "but" for "and" is what was needed, and now the mood change is clear. The sense of the second clause is not a continuation of the first, and the reader is not confused.

Here are some other mood changers (and note how one word can often do the work of an entire phrase): *however, still, therefore, yet, nevertheless, although, meanwhile*. As William Zinsser points out, "Always make sure that the reader is oriented." And make sure it's done without delay.

One of the more useful ways to warm up your writing is to remain in the first person—the "I" and "we" approach. It's the subjective point of view, and it establishes a bond between writer and reader because the writer is showing vulnerability. The writer opens herself to the reader, revealing those inner thoughts and feelings that a more objective writing style might not portray easily. Note the difference:

> I could only gasp at the sight of her broken body, as my mind played back the fragments of our childhood ...

> He could only gasp at the sight of her broken body, as his mind played back the fragments of their shared childhood ...

There's an immediacy in the first selection that's not present in the second. We can identify with the narrator more easily because it's as if the story is being related to us directly by the person who suffered these feelings, not by an uninvolved intermediary. We tend to identify more easily when the writer uses the first person, and this makes the writing warmer. "He says" ... "I say," "You went" ... "I went," "They heard" ... "We heard." The first person, singular or plural, brings the reader closer, and every writer strives for that.

The first person has limitations, though. While it will warm up most writing, it also restricts the writer to viewing things through that person's eye. Events, conversations, and feelings happening beyond the narrator's awareness are also beyond the writer's use. The first person requires a storyline that can't take in circumstances that could broaden things; everything must be compressed to the narrator's awareness. And the writer must face this dilemma early: Do you wish to emphasize warmth at the expense of story breadth, or can you write in the second or third person and still maintain that warmth? Are you experienced enough, is your story strong enough, to create that warmth without help from breadth of narrative scope?

Warm words flow from the strength of your convictions. A weak approach (uncertainty, passive verb forms, unimaginative modifiers) cools everything down, and the results can be uninspired prose—things become less personal, less involving ...

And you'll lose readers.

DON'T USE JOURNALESE OR SLANGIFY WORDS AND PHRASES

"Thanks for a fine write," wrote the editor of a national magazine to a contributor. "We expect to publish your story in our spring issue."

The author was pleased with the acceptance and never thought to wonder about the metamorphosis of the verb "write" until later. He showed the letter to an author friend, and the reaction to it was swift.

"A fine 'write'? How precious."

"I know what he means," said the contributor.

"Is he going to edit your piece?"

"Why shouldn't he?"

The friend had a dilemma. Writers should help other writers, especially when they seek constructive comment, but here, the friend sensed an edge of defensiveness. How much should he say?

"The editor's been on staff a while?"

"Years, I guess."

The friend shrugged; he might as well be frank. "The guy should know better."

"It's an acceptance letter, that's all."

"If he edits the way he writes letters, you've got problems…"

What the friend was referring to was the slip into "journalese" that the editor made. It's a form of writing that twists and turns parts of speech into demons that clutter up the page. It's a "quilt of instant words patched together out of other parts of speech," according to William Zinsser, and the result is laziness of expression

that can descend into cliché after cliché. Zinsser, in his *On Writing Well*, goes on: "This is a world where eminent people are 'famed' and their associates are 'staffers,' where the future is always 'upcoming' and someone is forever 'firing off' a note." It is shorthand writing at its most egregious, and it suffers from the same lack as any other shorthand: the words have little depth or substance; they are one-dimensional and offered to save space.

What if that editor had written: "Thanks for a fine piece of writing"? Or "Thanks for doing a fine article"? Or "Thanks for the good work"? Any of these would have provided the same message but without the self-conscious, twisted verb-into-noun. It's no different than if you take a shovel and try to make it do the work of a hammer. In the short run, it could probably be used this way, even though this is not what it's designed for. But eventually the shovel will break apart under the relentless pounding.

The tendency to use "journalese" is really an urge to be colloquial, to make your words and phrases understandable to the general public. The more you cut away the formality, the more you'll develop a bond with the reader, so the thinking goes. Newspaper and magazine people through the years have catered to a readership that wants easy reading because their studies and surveys have indicated that's what appeals to readers. There's a reason why the newspaper *USA Today* has been called "McPaper." Some readers don't want studied comment or literary flavor; they prefer plain vanilla prose quickly served.

This is fine *if*—a major if—as a writer, you don't kid yourself that you're offering something else. Go ahead and write "journalese" prose if the audience wishes it or expects it, but don't think that's the sort of writing most non-journalist writers are producing. A savvy writer has enough pride not to slink into lazy writing and to never be content with clichés.

The Watergate affair of the 1970s produced "journalese" from the political arena. Perhaps it was a peculiar reflection on those

in the Nixon Administration, brought on by their sense that nothing was beyond twisting, including their own language, but as awareness of wrongdoing grew and faces began to fit the shadows, we started to hear of "stonewalling" and "toughing it out." We knew what was meant, of course, but a figure of speech had been twisted, and a cliché had been born. (In fact, Watergate has become a "journalese" cliché of its own, spawning Irangate, Coingate, and others.)

We can produce the same sort of thing: "to green it up" for making things grow and develop, "to barber my hair" for allowing a barber to cut and trim, "to frost it over" for chilling an item until it develops a frost. These are verb mutants taken from another form of speech, usually a noun or adjective, and the grammatical effect is decidedly unremarkable. Such mutants don't make things clearer (as grammar is intended to do), and they tend to shortcut or interrupt any literary style (unless the entire style follows this "journalese" form, in which case we'd have a hard time calling the result literary).

Using "journalese" is a cheap way of achieving a result, and what it provides in clarity it takes back in freshness. How many times have you heard of someone "toughing it out" or "stonewalling" since the early 1970s? The phrases might have started out in the political arena, but it's a sure bet they've reappeared in sportsfare, militaryfare and social commentaryfare (and how about *those* examples of "journalese"!). The more a mutant word or phrase gets used, the more it ventures away from freshness toward becoming a cliché. There's no more condemning review than "he never met a cliché he didn't like." It is the most complete criticism of all because it means the writer has fallen back on overused words and phrasing and has not allowed the creative urge to bloom.

It isn't only verb mutants that wallow in "journalese." Adjectives can become nouns, too. A number of years ago *Time* maga-

zine followed a style that rode this type of writing to heights never achieved before. In an effort to be slick and quick they wrote of "greats" and "notables":

"An official list of the *greats* in magazine publishing includes…"

"The table of *notables* was set right under the dais…"

What's wrong with writing, "An official list of great magazine publishers includes…" or "The table of notable guests was set under the dais…"? Unquestionably, space has been saved with the "journalese," but the shorthand phrasing has added nothing to style. The best approach is to not twist a part of speech from one form into another. It may seem like a bit of a game to find new ways to use the words, but it results in lazy and inexact writing that has probably already been overused. "Don't let yourself get in this position," William Zinsser advises. "The only way to fight it is to care deeply about words."

There are also problems with writing slang, such as in this exchange:

"Okay, this is the deal, but don't bust a gut till you hear me out…"

"C'mon, knock it off!"

"Hey man! No hassles!"

"Don't blow your cool, man…"

When conversation becomes dialogue, a subtle distinction must be made. Conversation is spoken give-and-take, and all of us engage in it every day. But many conversations don't measure up when they are in writing. The reason is that what is conversation to the ear is not necessarily dialogue to the eye. Dialogue is conversation with *drama*, and this means that mere spoken words should not appear on the page unless *they have dramatic effect.* The reason is obvious: it's a story we're writing and drama must be part of it. A general conversation often has other purposes, and many times no one pays attention to dramatic effect.

Things are different between the world of the written word and the world of living experience. So it is with slang, that body of words and expressions that form an inescapable rim on our language, yet achieve so little respect. Slang, according to *Webster's Dictionary*, is "an informal nonstandard vocabulary composed typically of coinages, arbitrarily changed words, and extravagant, forced or facetious figures of speech." That's a lot of words to say something we already know. Slang is colloquialisms, sometimes with vulgar connotation.

Most of us have a good ear for slang—we know it when we hear it—and our vocabulary is sprinkled with it as we converse. In the short dialogue passage on the previous page, there's an over-abundance of slang, to be sure, but if the lines were to be spoken, they'd seem less awkward, more natural. On the page, however, they don't carry the same effect—they seem cliché-ridden (which they are) and self-conscious (which they are) and almost phony. As dialogue, the passage doesn't quite measure up.

That's one of the main problems with resorting to slang when you write. You know the effect you want, but the slang might turn the reader off (another slang phrase that could be better said another way). For some writers, "slangifying" prose is simply a reflection of reality. It is, after all, the way people talk! We use slang all the time. We can't get away from it.

The good writer knows better. The way people talk is *not* the way they should be portrayed on the written page. Dialogue is conversation with drama, remember?

Slang comes up repeatedly in my writing classes, and some students have a tough time with it. They think of slang the way an overzealous child might feed a goldfish: more is better. Unfortunately, it's exactly the opposite: less is better. Slang should be approached as an exotic condiment for a fine meal—a few drops at a time.

I recall a student who submitted a short story set in a bar. Her protagonist was fighting twin addictions—drugs and alco-

hol—and trying to preserve her relationship with a man who was attracted to another woman in the bar.

"I want to shoot up," she had her protagonist say. "Don't hassle me."

The bar was "smoke-filled" and "grubby" and "tough on the ears."

There were "cold ones" in front of some patrons and the "brew" was the popular brand. The man in question had "solid pectorals" in spite of a "beer gut" and he "smoked like a chimney."

It actually was not a bad story, but using so many slang words and expressions turned a credible job into an incredible one. She had lost me by the third paragraph. She had turned her prose into dull fare and her characters into blank faces, and I had no reason to feel anything.

That's the problem with "slangifying" prose. It does away with the vibrancy that comes naturally when you have fresh words and phrases; it makes them dull. Slang words are colloquialisms, which means they have been part of our language for a while and are readily used at all levels. It also means they tend to be overused and don't represent the most appealing choice. Would you use "bum" for a person who is homeless? "Beer-blast" for a college fraternity party? "Wheels" for an automobile? Slang words certainly convey a meaning, and the meaning might be proper within the context of the sentence or paragraph, but the problem is to integrate the slang into the rest of the prose so it doesn't disrupt the smoothness and the pace.

"These bums started out like you and me," she said. "They weren't homeless from birth."

"The college has a responsibility for regulating beer-blasts," the Dean said. "We must protect our students."

"The funeral cortege rounded the corner, and midway back were Harry and John's wheels, driven by Little Angie..."

You know what these sentences mean, and you know what the slang words are attempting to convey. The problem is that the slang doesn't fit in with the rest of the sentence; it disrupts the flow and injects a sour beat into the rhythm. No one wants that.

How do you recognize slang? It may sound obvious but ... listen to your conversations, because we all pepper slang throughout our day. We speak in colloquialisms, we even think (as we speak) in colloquialisms, and our listeners expect nothing more. "Pretty rambunctious today, aren't you?" you might say, and the slang needs no refinement. "It's a crap-shoot out there," and you understand what's meant. "This place is a dump." How many times have you said or thought that?

You need to activate your slang-antennae so you understand when you're tempted to use slang in your writing. Awareness is the key, not because slang doesn't have a place in all forms of communication, but because its place must be limited if you're going to produce smooth, flowing prose. Slang-awareness forces you to adopt a more creative writing approach because, like clichés, slang words reflect a certain laziness in application. It's easy to fall back on the slang description of an item, in the same way it's easy to rely on clichés. These are familiar words and phrases that require no arduous creative effort to recall. They may not fire up an image because they've been around too long and have passed beyond that stage. Slang projects a roughness, a coarseness that will affect the smoothness of the prose.

It reminds me of something that occurred during the height of the student protests in the late 1960s and early 1970s. At Columbia University in New York City, where some of the more violent protests took place, a meeting was held between the president of the University and some of the student protest leaders. Scrubbed, clean and well dressed, the university officials approached the meeting in business-like fashion, expecting a spirited but civilized give-and-take.

Not so the students. As the meeting opened, one of the student leaders removed his shoes and socks and proceeded to clean the dirty spaces between his toes. He continued to participate in the discussion while the officials felt a deep jarring blow to their sense of decorum.

Here was slang brought to real life. Coarseness amidst ample respectability. As an incident in an ongoing real-life confrontation, it had clear dramatic effect, but if you think of it in terms of writing technique, it could destroy a carefully constructed mood. Using slang with stylistic prose is no different than attempting to negotiate with Columbia University in bare feet.

Slang, however, does have a limited purpose in your writing, and even the most experienced writer would acknowledge it. Because slang words are colloquialisms, they reflect where the speaker (or writer) might have grown up or spent his time. For example, in Robert Reeves' mystery, *Peeping Thomas*, the protagonist, a college professor, prefers the seamy side of life in his off hours. He calls himself a "slummer" and some of his expressions are downright "slangy": "tuning in," "keeping to the straight and narrow," "ring a bell?" and "scuzzball."

It works well, though, because we *expect* these expressions from this type of character, and we're not put off when we see them. A lowlife (which is the way the character constantly refers to himself) would throw around slang expressions, and if he didn't, we might find him unrealistic. Even so, you still have to be careful not to overwhelm the reader because slang simply can't stand by itself. It's too one-dimensional.

Go back to the beginning of this section on slang. The dialogue could have been written better, and the first thing you'd do is remove most of the slang. Give it some style and honest creativity, and the reader could become intrigued:

"You're not going to like this ..."

"Bad news I don't have time for."

"No hassles, okay?

"I'm waiting..."

"I *said*..."

"Easy now."

Barely a slang expression here, and it picks up the reader more easily. A character can speak in slang, but when you portray him, make sure his slang doesn't take over.

You don't want the stuff to freak out and rile the reader.

Dig me?

DON'T OVERUSE
THE THESAURUS

It dares you to flip it open and solve your dilemma. You need a word, one word, one simple word, so close, a nudge is all you want.

Then a powerful calm as you pull the one-and-a-half-inch thick volume from the shelf and notice the bold statement on the title page (in some cases it's printed on the cover itself): THE RIGHT WORD AT THE RIGHT TIME.

The thesaurus!

You search ... and search ... and search ... and that simple word remains elusive. Nothing seems quite appropriate, even though you find words you hadn't thought about in years. You rerun your sentence through your mind, sliding word after word in, then sliding word after word out, never satisfied with the fit. The choices surround you with their variety and their urgings, and you know you have to decide: one of these, or a new search, or perhaps the word that had first flown into your mind before you opened the book?

Writers through the generations have used the thesaurus; no self-respecting English major or journalist would be without one. The crucial question, however, isn't *if* the thesaurus is useful, but *how* useful, and the answer goes a long way to portraying your own independent mind-set. Because there's no doubt (at least in this corner) that the thesaurus is valuable and useful, that it can add to anyone's prose, and can take a writer to places her mind had decided it did not wish to go.

But the thesaurus is not a magic wand; it cannot answer every word-problem; it cannot turn dross phrasing into shiny-gold poetry. What it can do it does well, but in the process, it can fool you into thinking that its grasp exceeds its reach. After all, there's that undiluted claim on the title page: THE RIGHT WORD AT THE RIGHT TIME!

And anyway, as humans and writers we're continually seeking a formula for easing this arduous creative process. What's better than a handy reference that spreads the choices before us?

Unfortunately, creativity and the creative process aren't so neatly developed. Finding the right word isn't like picking green jellybeans from a many-colored sea of candy. We weigh and analyze and *feel*; the fit must be right, and so a dry, one-dimensional formula that tries to give us THE RIGHT WORD AT THE RIGHT TIME does not always work.

There's no doubt the thesaurus has a long and honored history (Roget published his first edition in 1852), and its value is attested to by its continued and widely recognized use. But beware: There is a trap in putting too much value on this highly respected volume. For its usefulness to writers, the thesaurus can exact a solid price.

The trouble comes if you begin to take that undiluted claim — THE RIGHT WORD AT THE RIGHT TIME — to heart and rely upon it to the exclusion of your creative instinct. You may begin to see the thesaurus as an absolute support instead of a relative one; you might turn to it over and over whenever the slightest uncertainty about wording or phrasing develops, and gradually abdicate your thoughtful independence by adopting the word lists on the pages. You may come to rely on the thesaurus *too much*.

And because it offers a dry compilation without creative connections, your writing could become mechanical and uninspired. Not all the right words are in the thesaurus, though most of them

are. It is better to seek such words with a jaundiced eye—it *might* be here, then again, it might not be—and to expect the thesaurus to fail you from time to time.

Another danger with the thesaurus is that it seems so "official," and you may come to treat it as a sort of final arbiter. Nothing could be further from the truth. It is printed and published by a private company, and it bears no stamp declaring it "official" anything. But in its arresting hardcover with its word lists carefully organized and its entries lengthy and encompassing (plus its bold claim: THE RIGHT WORD AT THE RIGHT TIME), it carries itself with solid authority, and an uncertain writer (which most of us are) could be excused for assuming it is unimpeachable.

But note its limitations: it does not tell you which word you must use in which situation (except that it does provide the noun, verb, adjective, and adverb forms of the words on the lists); it does not provide *complete* word lists, because our language is always evolving; and it can force you into some strange choices.

Yes, strange choices. Let's follow the thesaurus's depiction of *writer*. Here's what mine offers:

> ... author, litterateur, homme de letters, essayist, journalist, publicist, scribe, penman, war (special) correspondent, pen, scribbler, the scribbling race, ghost, hack, literary hack, Grub-street writer ... reporter, penny-a-liner, editor, subeditor, literary agent ...

How often do we call ourselves scribes? Or Grub-street writers? Yet they are on the list, and to the more literal among us, if it's on the list, there must be "official" approval for it somewhere.

That's where the danger comes in. Merely because it's on the list doesn't mean it's appropriate (and it's easy to pick the *wrong* word, too; remember, the thesaurus doesn't give definitions). So you should approach these word lists as you approach a strange dog whose tail wags slowly: friendly, yes, but first with gentle words before extending a hand and arm.

A friend of mine had received a communications degree in college, and after a couple of years putting out a well-received newsletter, she decided to try freelancing as a fiction writer. She bought herself a new desk, a new chair, a new computer, the spiffiest letterhead paper and envelopes … and a new thesaurus, along with a dictionary and the latest *Writer's Market*. If anyone could be ready, it was she.

The only problem was she had written little fiction, and she had only a vague idea what she wanted to write about. "Oh, well," she told me. "Whenever I've been stuck, the thesaurus has usually bailed me out. I'm sure it will with fiction, too."

But, of course, it didn't because writing newsletter copy and writing fiction are two different things. A couple of months after she began, I received a call. She was in tears. "I'm so frustrated!" she cried. "Nothing I write has any life. It's dull."

I started to suggest ways she could build up her drama, when she burst out: "The thesaurus was no help either! All those words, I wanted to scream."

She found out the hard way: the thesaurus is not a magic wand.

It can save us time, though, and sometimes this can make *anything* worthwhile. A word is on the edge of your mind, you can make out its letter sounds, you know what connotation you seek, but you can't quite grasp it … Here the thesaurus will be a reliable friend. Go into the index at the back and find the word list for the connotation you must satisfy, then go to that word list and read the various choices. Somewhere in there you'll find what you're looking for. Guaranteed.

William Zinsser calls the thesaurus a "bulging grab-bag" and he warns not to give in to hilarity merely because you come across some tortured words that went out of favor when knighthood went out of flower. "There is no better friend to have around to nudge your memory," he says. "You should use it with gratitude."

But temper gratitude with reality. Relying on the thesaurus too much can make you mentally lazy and blunt creativity. In the human quest for solutions, it can become more important to get a word or phrase down on paper (you completed the search, you've *found* something) than to assure yourself that the fit is proper. That sort of attitude is only for those who can afford to be insensitive to the flavors of words; you rise and fall with the *right* word, not just *a* word.

So, by all means, use the thesaurus, but think of it as an aid, not an answer.

Or as William Zinsser says: "The thesaurus is to the writer what the rhyming dictionary is to the songwriter—a reminder of all the choices ..."

No, not *all* the choices. Most of them, though.

8

DON'T UNDERUSE
THE DICTIONARY

Some writers are blessed (or cursed) with monumental egos, and they find it difficult to admit their limitations. Perhaps it's because they deal in a product—words—that can't be quantified by height, width and breadth as, say, an automobile or a piece of real estate. Words transcend three-dimensional reality, and this offers a chance to assume rarified thrones of authority.

Who better knows words (say some writers) and how to use them? Who better *understands* the language?

That monumental ego. It jumps in the way, and when it does, something gets lost, usually a better spin on a word or phrase. Some writers simply don't give the dictionary the respect it deserves, and inevitably, the misstep will show in their writing. The attitude resembles that of the adolescent who avoids babysitting because Mom and Dad have always provided an allowance. The moment of truth comes when the allowance is turned off, and the adolescent has no way to acquire that extra-special, most important, awesome CD she desperately needs.

Only then does the value of babysitting strike home.

Writers who don't use the dictionary, or who don't use it much, never really see what they've missed because they assume that what they need is between their ears. The moment of truth will strike when the copyeditor's blue pencil (assuming the manuscript reaches this stage) challenges wording or phrasing the writer feels

at ease with, or when a rejection slip arrives with a cryptic comment referring to "style" or "usage."

A writer needs to think of his work as a delicately crafted pyramid, where each word must fit with every other word, where a word or phrase out of balance will reflect on the entire structure. The dictionary is the trowel for properly setting the bricks that become our words. Misuse it, or ignore it, and nothing will seem to fit.

One evening when I was about ten years old, my father walked into my room while I was reading and gestured at the books piled on my bed.

"Ever try reading the dictionary?" he asked.

I recall my reaction was similar to being asked to sip cod liver oil, and I fought the suggestion with some vehemence.

"It's not what you think," he said. "Try reading a single page, no more than that."

"The dictionary's boring," I said. "I like stories."

"Every word has its own story," he said.

Reluctantly, I flipped to the M's, and the first word that hit my eye was *minor, adj [ME.fr.L. smaller, inferior]* ... I wondered what the abbreviations were for because I knew the word referred to me. I was a minor; I had heard people talk of me this way. My eye trailed down the page, and there were words I recognized: *mint, minuet, minus, minute* ... I sensed a familiarity that I hadn't expected, as if this thick, forbidding volume had warmth and coziness once opened. I looked up to see my father smiling.

"When I was your age, I was reading the dictionary almost every night," he said.

"There's so much to memorize," I said.

He shook his head. "Read it as you would a story. Each word has its own plot, see how it developed."

No one at school would believe this, that I knew!

But I did begin to read the dictionary, and as my father predicted, I came to see the story in each word, its root, its

progression through the ages, its shades of meaning. In time I came to value my dictionary as highly as I would any adolescent geegaw, and I knew I could retreat to it for unvaried certainty. It was a place where I could be sure of truth and where I could always find a story.

It's surprising how few people really know what's in the dictionary. For ready reference I use *Webster's Seventh New Collegiate Dictionary*, which is based on *Webster's Third New International Dictionary*, and even here, in abridged form, there is a wealth of material. Of course, the words themselves comprise the bulk of this volume, but look at some of the special features:

—a guide to pronunciation

—a list of common abbreviations, including symbols for chemical elements

—common proofreader's marks (especially useful when editors have a go at your manuscript and don't translate their marks). There's even a marked up copy of Lincoln's Gettysburg Address to see how it's done.

—more than five thousand biographical names, along with proper pronunciations

—a pronouncing gazetteer (a geographical listing, including population) of more than ten thousand locations around the world

There's other information, too, including the rules on punctuation, common spelling approaches, and a vocabulary of rhymes that "are in keeping with the practice of poets who observe traditional rules of rhyming." It should be clear that the dictionary is much more than a list of words and their meanings. It serves a number of purposes, and it helps in a number of ways.

Though, of course, it is the words and their meanings you turn to first. Look at what you can find from one simple entry. Take a word of great significance to us all: *author*

... *n* [ME *auctour*, fr. ONF, fr. L *auctor* fr. promoter, originator, author, fr. *auctus* pp of *augere* to increase — more at EKE] ...

This is but the etymology of the word, its history, its story. You haven't even arrived at the meanings yet. The dictionary states that it intends to trace a word back as far as it can in English language — to go back to our language roots — and here then is the story. You find that *author* is a noun from a Middle English word, *auctor*, that meant promoter, originator, author, which in turn was derived from the Latin word, *auctus*, the past participle of the Latin verb, *augere*, meaning to increase. And then if this isn't enough, you're directed to the symbol EKE, which gives you Old English and, surprise! Old High German roots for the friendly Latin verb, *augere*, to increase.

All of this, and you haven't reached the up-to-date meanings yet. But what you have found out is that there's a story behind the word we use to define ourselves, that authoring, at least in the old days, meant promoting as well as creating. (To bring in modern perspective, there is Truman Capote's breezy advice: "A boy's got to hustle his book.") *Author*, then, has a long, rich history, and it has sprung from several roots and cultures; it exhorts us to increase, to make something more of what we have.

Somehow, it makes me feel better to know this.

The dictionary is really the best place to get a current reading on our language. The newest slang probably won't appear until it has proven its staying power, but that's not to say the dictionary is stodgy or unimaginative. In fact, some years ago the editors of *American Heritage* decided to produce a brand new dictionary, and they assembled a "panel on usage," a group of writers, editors and academics who would guide the project. One of the choices involved the word "bed." A decision was made to provide the verb form and meaning ("to bed her/him ..."), since the free-thinking 1960s had come and gone, the mania for turning nouns into verbs had followed, and common usage was quite extensive. So *The American Heritage Dictionary* was published, and then came the surprise. A school district in Alaska objected to the usage (to be

fair, there were several other words that also carried erotically-inspired meanings), and the dictionary was banned from schools.

But all was not lost. The editors of *American Heritage* probably consoled themselves that at least their work rested on the cutting edge of our language. If a dictionary is to be valuable, it must stay current, and certainly *The American Heritage Dictionary* qualified in Alaska.

What the dictionary does for us is to offer a leg up on syntax—the orderly arrangement of words and phrases. A writer with sloppy syntax is usually an unpublished writer because awkward phrasing turns editors off. The dictionary gives the part of speech (noun, verb, adjective, adverb), as well as its extensions. For example, take the adjective *hateful*: following its meaning, we see *hatefully* (the adverb) and *hatefulness* (the noun). There are even some synonyms provided, along with meanings for each, showing the shades of difference between them. Proper syntax would use *hateful* as an adjective; improper syntax would use it as a noun or adverb without adding an "ly" or "ness" ending, thus bringing on awkward phrasing that editors cringe over.

We also avoid tripping over words that *seem* to carry the same meaning but are different, too. The dictionary can give us the precision of a laser so we can distinguish. Are *story* and *tale* the same? Many times we use them interchangeably, and in my dictionary *story* is "an account of incidents or events" and *tale* is "a relation of a series of events or facts." Not much difference there. But further on, *story* is also "the intrigue or plot of a narrative or dramatic work" and *tale* is "an improper report of a private or confidential matter." These closely related words diverge here, and the dictionary helps you decide which will fit exactly with what you wish to say.

It is with word meanings that the dictionary is most useful. For writers the important thing is to reach for help *before* making assumptions about meanings. That ego can get in the way as you tell yourself *I know that!* when in fact you're quite vague about the meaning. Ask the hard question: do I *really* know the meaning of this word, that phrase? Don't assume. The dictionary offers two or three meanings for each entry, and it also shows the proper grammar approach. You can pick and choose among meanings, but at least you'll be able to judge whether the word or phrase you wish to use is the right one.

Every published writer I know uses the dictionary on a regular basis. Not a day goes by that I don't refer to it, and I consider it my best friend. As with any friend there are times when we don't see eye to eye, and there are times when it plain disappoints me. But I trust my dictionary, and I know that in my writer's heart-of-hearts it protects my best interests. It does what no other volume of reference work can do: it gives me the "essence" of use for grammar and syntax. Without it, I'd be navigating on a horizonless desert.

And it's easy to use, too!

9

DON'T DUCK THE PUNCH IN PUNCTUATION

There's a little book we used when we were in junior high school: *The Rules of Punctuation* ... or maybe *Punctuation and Your Writing* ... or perhaps *How to Punctuate a Sentence* ... It was our introduction to that ordered world of commas and semicolons and periods and all the other punctuation marks that turn unfinished prose into polished writing. The title of the little book doesn't matter, but I remember those early experiences with punctuation because here is where the formality in my writing took shape. I discovered there were rules for using commas ("where three or more elements are in a series, they should be separated ..."); there were rules for semicolons ("when the two independent parts of a compound sentence are not joined by a conjunction ..."); and there were rules for the other marks, as well. I came to see punctuation as integral to whatever I wrote and for good reason; it brought clarity and natural rhythm, and it allowed readers to enjoy what I wrote. No more confusion, no more misunderstanding, the rules for punctuation would help me.

Yet, these still were *rules*, and that meant rigidity and limits. There was good punctuation and bad punctuation, and the dividing line seemed to rest on ease of reading. If it promoted *that*, it was good punctuation.

Most of us probably learned the rules by rote and never gave a thought to how or why the rules were there in the first place.

The one other thing we probably didn't learn is that punctuation is a lot more than commas, semicolons, and periods, and when used with imagination and decisiveness, punctuation can add immeasurable zest to our writing. Punctuation beefs up style, and an experienced writer knows how to make the most of it.

Take the simple dash (—) for instance. The chances are most of us didn't learn how to use the dash when we learned The Rules of Punctuation, yet here is a mark that can serve so many purposes. In *The Chicago Manual of Style* (which most authors and editors use) look at how it is denoted:

> "[as] a sudden break in thought that causes an abrupt change in sentence structure ..."

> "to indicate interruptions in or breaks in faltering speech ..."

> "to give emphasis or explanation by expanding a phrase occurring in the main clause ..."

And there are many more. The simple dash has multiple uses, not least of which is to turn a soggy phrase into one with life. A dash can create tension in the same way that short, snappy phrases or harsh, active verbs can. It can force a level of excitement upon the reader by graphic technique:

> He tiptoed across the hall—there! Suddenly, a crocodile face ...

The narrative switches abruptly from stealthy movement to explosive action, and the dash works like the flashbulb in a darkroom. All is at low hum, a certain intensity is present, but it's not diverting. Then BANG! ... SMASH! ... WOW! ... and the action becomes explosive, the intensity balloons. Why? Because a face suddenly appears. Read the sentence without the dash and notice the level of intensity drop. Try inserting a comma for the dash, try a period, or begin a new sentence with "suddenly."

It simply doesn't work as well. The dash makes it go, and the reason is the dash creates abruptness in a way no other mark can. It resembles a stop sign that emerges from the mist. The reader

can't see it until he is almost upon it, and that's one of its virtues. It changes perspectives immediately, and it can create a sharp turn in the action.

Abruptness is the key, tension the result, and good writing the beneficiary.

Dashes, however, can work the other way, as well. Suppose we want to slow things down, *reduce* the tension level?

> He was a man with secrets—secrets, that is, he had shared judiciously—and people seemed to make allowances for that...

Here the dashes set off a subordinate clause that helps to explain the main clause. It adds emphasis, and it does so with some force, but the tension level subsides because the subordinate clause is explanatory, not excitement-building. If we had used commas instead of dashes, the entire sentence might have read awkwardly because the subordinate clause is strong enough to stand—almost—on its own, and commas would have weakened it substantially. But note this too: Using the dashes provides a pause in the action, and this has the effect of giving the reader a breather. It's especially significant if the prior paragraphs have been filled with tension. In this instance, the dashes act as yellow caution lights instead of stop signs, but they do change the speed the reader has been traveling.

How about the mark we call the ellipsis? It's usually three dots at the end of a sentence or a clause (...) and stands for the omission of a word or phrase, line or paragraph. Until Tom Wolfe began using it regularly in his nonfiction in the 1960s, the ellipsis was more a creature of academia than anything else. In scholarly papers, we'd read a quoted passage, and the author would skip certain words or phrases that had little relevance to what was being quoted.

But not anymore. Tom Wolfe popularized the ellipsis and showed it had dramatic purpose. Now we can use it to build tension:

> He opened the door... God, it was dark in there... blackness like tar... smelly too... a tiny flutter of air...

Try writing this with commas where the ellipsis points are, then read it over. It doesn't seem so intense, now. The reason is that ellipsis points force the unsettling events ("blackness like tar … smelly, too …") to be spread out, to have a longer effect than if the phrases come one after the other, separated only by a comma. And because the effect is spread, the tension can develop with more power.

Some think the ellipsis should be used only to indicate a pause in the dialogue or narrative ("I'm so tired tonight but I do remember …"), but this curtails some of the ellipsis' most telling effect. It is a tension builder, and it can add punch to any sentence or paragraph.

> He was tired … or was he? Forty-eight hours with no sleep … he couldn't remember saying his name … did they ask? They had to know … maybe they didn't care.

If these clauses had been run together, using commas perhaps, or making them into short, complete sentences, the effect would not be so strong. It is the ellipsis that strings out the action and builds the excitement. This is not a pause in the narrative to slow things down, but rather to speed them up, because each clause following an ellipsis changes the direction of the prose; it doesn't simply continue it.

> He was tired … *or was he?*
>
> He couldn't remember … *did they ask?*
>
> They had to know … *maybe they didn't care.*

This is the key: When the prose direction is changed—whether with dialogue or narrative—and an ellipsis is used, tension will build. The punctuation will add punch.

The same is true with using capitalization. ALL CAPS ADD EMPHASIS TO SIGHT AND SOUND. THE WORDS

SCREAM OUT AT THE READER, CLUTCH HIM BY THE
THROAT, AND SHAKE.

Which of the following is more eye-catching:

"HELP! ... I'M DROWNING ... !"

"Help! ... I'm drowning ... !"

Obviously, the first line is more graphic. Using all capitalization
gives words and phrases a boldness no other form of emphasis can
match. Underline, italics, even an ellipsis won't arrest attention
quite as readily as all caps. The effect, of course, is to explode the
action, to detonate an event, and you would certainly have the
reader's attention. But be careful: All caps should be used cau-
tiously, only a few words at any one time. If the technique is used
too often or with too many words in a series, the effect wears off.
It works only when the reader doesn't expect it. If half the book
is in all caps, the reader wouldn't think the type size unusual, and
the special effect would be lost.

All caps have another use, too. In addition to providing emphasis (and thereby raising tension), it can also show major dis-
comfort or unsettledness. Here's how:

RUNTHEWORDSTOGETHERANDTHEYPROJECTPANICANDCONFUSION ...

Persons in this state of mind might certainly run words (or
thoughts) together because they themselves are out of control.
Using lowercase might get the mental state across, but using all
caps will get it across with explosive force, and the effect occurs
because there is no pause between the words—everything rushes
on. It's the same thing as uttering words without a breath; eventually things will fall apart. You need to catch your breath—in
conversation or on the written page—if you wish to modulate
the atmosphere.

But if you wish to pack a punch with your punctuation, hold-
ing your breath could be the best solution.

DON'T WALLOW IN A SENTENCE STRAIGHTJACKET

"Variety's the very spice of life," as the poet William Cowper once observed. Never is that more apt than when applied to how we write. Prose sentences that resemble cookie-cutter models (same size, same order, same surface, same interior), line after line, offer no variety, and hence no excitement, no spice.

Writers who fall into the trap like this become wrapped in a sentence straightjacket.

> The day was cold and raw. It snowed a little. The barn walls had peeling green paint. The hay bales were stacked up. The old car was on blocks by the door...

Note the sameness of these sentences, their length, their rhythm, their ingredients. For a short paragraph, perhaps, the writer might get away with it, but suppose this type of writing went on and on, page after page? It would become so repetitive as to dull the reader's reactions, and we know what happens next.

Thud! The book is closed...

Call it sentence sameness, if you're in an alliterative mood, but the result can destroy creative expression. The more identical the sentences, the less imaginative the expression can be.

Naturally, you don't need to write this way, but the tendency to fall into the habits awaits us all. Why? Because you can get lazy, and you may find it less arduous to stamp out sentence-clones than to work and try to vary things. Making sure you avoid the sentence straightjacket is *work* because you have to be aware of

your rhythms and procedures. You have to weigh your writing continually; you have to ask yourself, "Am I setting things up too rigidly?" … "Do my sentences run the same length with the same style and order?" … "Have I dropped into the trap?"

Take a look at this short passage from William Faulkner's *Light in August*:

> McEachern lay in bed. The room was dark, but he was not asleep. He lay beside Mrs. McEachern, whom he did believe to be sleeping, thinking fast and hard, thinking. 'The suit has been worn. But when. It could not have been during the day, because he is beneath my eyes, except on Saturday afternoons …'

There's variety in pace and rhythm here. Each sentence is different in length and scope from every other one. There are five sentences all together, and only one is declarative ("McEachern lay in bed"). The others vary from interrogatory ("But when") to compound ("The room was dark, but he was not asleep") to conditional and hybrid declarative. The fact that they are all different from one another means simply this: *The reader can't be lulled to boredom because of sentence structure.* The variety in the ways the sentences are constructed gives life to the prose.

Now note the difference in the following two passages:

> The day was cloudy, and he was depressed. The wind blew, and he watched the tree branches whipsaw about. The ground was soggy, and he could feel water through his soles …

> The day was cloudy. Lord, he was depressed. Tree branches whipsawing in the cold wind, soggy earth under his porous shoes, not an ounce of comfort here …

Both passages offer essentially the same narrative, but the second one adds variety in sentence structure. The first passage is one compound sentence after another, and if this continued down the page, you'd find yourself seeking relief elsewhere. Not so with the

second passage where you've combined the sentences and made one complete sentence and one sentence fragment (remember how we gave life to fragments in Chapter 1?).

Once again, the key is to think of reaching the reader's *ear*, to write so that the reader can pick up the rhythm and be taken with it. A monotonous rhythm will produce monotonous writing, while an exciting, varied rhythm will result in more interesting writing. One way to do this is to vary not only types of sentences but important words *within* sentences.

Such as verb forms. For example, using the active voice makes your prose more dynamic; it speeds things up (for more on how and why this happens, see Chapter 21). Yet even the most active of active verb voices loses punch when it is one more in a long line of identical verb forms, paragraph after paragraph, page after page. If you read "He exploded ..." or "He demanded ..." or "He leapt up ..." without variation, you'd soon lose the edge of excitement the writer worked so hard to develop. A paragraph with nothing but the active voice works fine if it's action you're trying to highlight:

> The skier swished over the crest, his skis chattering across the ice granules the morning sun had yet to melt. He pumped his arms for added speed, and he shouted his enthusiasm into the cavernous morning cold ...

But keep this up for half a dozen paragraphs, and it would cease to be exciting. The sentence straightjacket trap would have sprung.

Instead, vary the verb voice. Use the passive form once in a while, even when there's action to be portrayed. The change of pace won't hurt the effect, provided it hasn't been overdone.

> The skier swished over the crest, his skis chattering across the ice granules that had not been melted by the morning sun. Speed was increased by pumping his arms, and he shouted his enthusiasm ...

The action isn't really slowed by the verb voice, but the prose is less uniform, and in the long run, that's what's important.

The same kind of thing can be done with paragraphing. As with sentences, you don't want to fall into the habit of writing paragraphs that develop the same length. This happens sometimes in journalism, where columnists write paragraph-clones with the identical number of sentences paragraph after paragraph.

The real problem comes when you're not aware that you're writing the same length paragraph. As it is with other straight-jacket traps, you can be caught without realizing it. There's but one thing to do—you must remain sensitized to all aspects of your writing. You must continually examine not only the kinds of sentences you're using, but their arrangement in paragraphs and exactly how your paragraphs themselves are arrayed.

The demands of style might push you into a sentence straight-jacket *deliberately*. That is, you may write uniform sentences or uniform paragraphs because you wish to get across a monolithic style, such as the way some writers did it in the nineteenth century. Balzac could spend four pages describing a room with sentence after sentence about the same length, but his purpose was to act as a camera, missing nothing. The uniform style contributed to this because it focused attention on all the details in the room; it didn't attempt to dramatize one item or collection of items at the expense of others.

Style, however, should never be used as an *excuse* for a sentence straightjacket. Style must blend in with the material; it must give purpose to the words and phrases; it must have the required effect. For example, a series of lengthy sentences offered to slow the action down works fine, until it's time for the action to speed up. Style would then dictate shortening the sentences—perhaps even the paragraphs—in order to pump up the effect.

Style is important here, but what's even more important is your awareness that a sentence straightjacket can become style. If you know you're doing it, you have the advantage.

But if you're unconscious about it, woe to your prose.

11

DON'T WRITE THE PERFECT PARAGRAPH

Remember the wagging finger of your eighth-grade teacher, and the textbook that drilled you on The Rules of Grammar, and the strange configurations on the blackboard that showed you how to "diagram" a sentence? Proper writing at that level was the product of rules and procedures, and you could be forgiven if, somehow, you got the impression that what you wrote took a backseat to how you wrote it.

What you learned—and what you may still be saddled with—is the inclination to write the perfect paragraph. Grammatically correct, substantively unambiguous and chronological, it is something an eighth-grade teacher could applaud. It proceeds from a "lead" sentence, then offers a step-by-step story buildup. The perfect paragraph violates none of the grammar rules, and it resonates with shining purity. The sentences are complete, punctuation marks properly inserted, subjects and predicates aligned, antecedents clearly defined. The perfect paragraph has everything covered … except style.

And that is the crucial element. Perfection without style is no perfection at all. Have you ever been attracted to someone from afar, only to find that appeal dissolve as you learn more about the inner person? Writing style is like that; it is the inner soul of the words on the page, it is what drives us to continue reading. A perfect paragraph without style loses everything; it becomes only an exercise.

Some writers have trouble with this—some editors, too. Once, I signed a contract to co-author a nonfiction book on the art of ballet. I understood the audience, mainly young dancers in the mid to late teens, and I knew that the way something was presented to them was as important as what was presented. If they didn't enjoy reading our words, then they wouldn't bother reading our book. In spite of deep dedication to their art, these young people were used to being entertained and to entertaining others. They were not used to uninspired prose.

I could see that style would be important in a book of this nature, even though it would get into the details of their art. My co-author, a dancer and teacher, agreed with me. I debated the unadorned journalistic approach with an offering of facts and uncomplicated explanations, and perhaps an occasional quote from some authority in the field. But as I played the idea through my mind, I could see *dull ... dull ... dull* flashing with neon certitude. Nonfiction written this way had the flavor of the lecture hall, and teenaged dancers were not inclined to sit still for that.

What was needed, I decided, was a style that offered more drama, more excitement. I was going to have to "break" some of the rules in order to write an interesting book. The important thing was for people to read it, not to admire its so-called perfection.

So I called up some of those drama-producing techniques we've already touched on (and some we'll get to later), and the book seemed to write itself. Among other things, I avoided long paragraphs; I stressed anecdotes and incidents (figuring a story within a story is always enticing); I kept my prose warm with contractions and ellipses; and I sometimes deliberately wrote incomplete sentences and short one-phrase paragraphs. My purpose was to keep the reader *involved*, and one good way of doing this was to speed everything up, to generate excitement and action (remember, my audience was dramatically inclined, highly motivated teenagers).

My co-author—who had supplied me with much of the technical information but had allowed me a free hand with style—was delighted with the results. "I've never read a ballet book quite like this," she said.

Off went the manuscript to the publisher, and we waited for reaction. Initially, not much was said, but then copyedited portions began to come back for revision, and I noticed that most of the ellipses, as well as many of the techniques I had used to avoid the perfect paragraph, were deleted or changed. The entire style of the book was under attack, and what was emerging was another dull old ballet book.

We pressed the editor for an explanation, and here's what she wrote: "There are grammatical errors in this manuscript ... Specifically, I refer to run-on sentences, one-sentence paragraphs ..."

"Don't you understand the dramatic effect of what's being done here?" we asked.

I pointed out that run-on sentences had the purpose of continuing a thought without the niceties of subject and predicate, that it was more lifelike, thus more personal to the reader and more identifiable. I argued that one-sentence paragraphs (which, of course, are *not* perfect paragraphs) develop action and excitement because the thought or the point of view changes so rapidly. "It's drama!" I underscored.

In the end the editor came around—partially. She saw her insistence on the perfect paragraph as too rigid, and she agreed to reinstate many of the items she had edited out. Who was finally vindicated? Well, the book became a book club selection, and the reviews were complimentary.

Take a look at some well-known fiction writers. Are they bogged down in writing the perfect paragraph? Ernest Hemingway, whose sense of craftsmanship was legendary, wasn't so hemmed in. In "The Snows of Kilimanjaro," his marvelous tale of hunting and death in Africa, he has his protagonist thinking:

> She shot very well this good, rich bitch, this kindly caretaker and de-
> stroyer of his talent. Nonsense. He had destroyed his talent himself...

And five lines later:

> What was this? A catalogue of old books?
>> What was his talent anyway?

In the perfect paragraph there are no incomplete sentences, all the grammar rules are followed. But see how Hemingway ignores this: one sentence has one word—*Nonsense*. Another sentence has five words: *A catalogue of old books?* Neither has subject nor predicate, neither would satisfy the grammar police.

But style benefits. The character is thinking, and we all know our thoughts don't operate with grammatical purity—we think in fits and starts. Incomplete sentences are often the result...and they give a realistic portrayal to the prose.

Or take a look at Larry McMurtry. In his novel, *Some Can Whistle*, about a highly successful, deeply depressed former television writer, one-sentence paragraphs appear from time to time (but never too frequently). Here is his narrator describing a nostalgic visit to a Houston neighborhood and to some of his deceased daughter's friends:

> Always, when in Houston, I drifted over to the Lawndale area, an Asian barrio by this time. The Mr. Burger was gone, replaced by a spiffy little restaurant called The Wok.
>> Sometimes I visited Sue Lin; she and her husband owned a computer store, staffed mainly by their lively children.
>> I tried to find Dew, but no one knew where Dew had gone.
>> Apart from having a larger Asian barrio...

Two straight one-sentence paragraphs in a row! Surely the grammar police would find that objectionable; surely that editor who took issue with our style in the ballet book would be offended. To her, a one-sentence paragraph was a "grammati-

cal error," but as you can see, it serves to develop a distinctive style, instead.

The perfect paragraph is an illusion, really. Striving to produce it will only create frustration for anyone seeking to develop true writing style. The key—as in so many instances—is to ask yourself the purpose of what you're trying to accomplish. The perfect paragraph may satisfy some age-old list of writing commandments, but, standing alone, it will not enhance readability.

What readers want is something that will touch them and hold them, and if you bow to the wagging finger of the grammar police, you'll find yourself cited for good citizenship ... while wondering where all the readers have gone.

And if you want the essence of variety, try the one-word paragraph. *That* will catch the reader.

Absolutely.

12

Don't Get Tricky and Jazzy With Style

In the catalogue description for many college writing courses there's one phrase that appears over and over ... the student "will learn to develop a 'personal voice'..."

Sounds a bit precious, sort of *literary* in that turned-up-nose manner. But, actually, it means pretty much what it says ... and it offers the clearest picture of the goal every writer should strive to attain.

Take the question, "Do the trains run on time?" In the hands of a realist, the answer might read:

"Of course. Our computer-switching equipment is state-of-the-art."

But in the hands of a romantic, it might read:

"The trains? Is it important? The wheel spin seems so ... timeless."

Each of us has a "personal voice," something that is unique to the way we look at things. If we're talented enough, we can have more than one personal voice, but that doesn't happen much. Down deep enough in our core, we have a way of looking at things that's so personal no one else could quite assume it. It's our bed-rock point of view, nurtured through genetics and environment to control the way we take in our world. For some of us, it might be a realistic approach; for others, it might be a romantic approach (because there's really no limit on this—there are as many "personal voices" as there are persons to have them). What you

write reflects your "personal voice"; it is your way of looking at material and presenting it.

So a writer with a more realistic bent might treat the same subject, even the same sentence, differently from one who is romantically inclined. This is the way your "personal voice" speaks, and it distinguishes you from every other writer.

But outside creative writing class, we rarely talk of "personal voice"; instead we speak of style, of the manner in which we present our material. Yet "personal voice" is the key ingredient in style because it is what singles you out; it is what makes you "different."

It is also what can make you fall on your face. Developing a personal writing style is certainly to be encouraged, but there can be too much of anything. If, in your zeal, you conjure prose mannerisms or idiosyncratic phrasing more for the sake of being different than because they represent your true "personal voice," the results become pretentious and distracting. Your writing style becomes stiff, and the readers will walk away.

Grammar is one way you can influence style or your "personal voice." But it must be carefully used, and it must have a purpose. It does nothing for you to develop an exotic style without being clear about the effect you wish it to have on the reader. And you must understand that the trickier, the jazzier you mold your style, the greater the risk that you'll turn off the reader.

I had a student once who showed great creative promise. He loved the narrative poets such as T.S. Eliot and Ezra Pound, and he saw himself producing this kind of work—but with a distinctive style. He submitted a manuscript on the theme of society's materialistic faces, and after opening with a quote from Heidegger, he began:

> someone shot our innocence in the back
> someone untied our net,
> knots fresh from a mesh wire net

and
the
rare colors ran
racing ahead of my reaction
off to the great sleep ...

Periodically, for the remainder of the tale (which ran more than six pages) he would juxtapose lengthy narrative with poetic flair such as above. It was, clearly, a highly distinctive style. I asked him two questions about the opening:

"Why the strange paragraphing?"

He shrugged. "Seemed different, I guess."

"Is the reader to conclude anything from what you've written?"

He laughed. "I never got beyond my own reaction."

I pressed him to think about it further, to consider what he would have a reader imagine when the words appeared on the page. He stared at his work, then he began to cross off the passage.

"Wait," I said ...

"No, no," he responded, flipping the pages. "That belongs *here!*" And he inserted the passage on page five. Then he rearranged the paragraphing so each line began at the left margin.

"I like my words," he said, "but I have a better opening now. And," he smiled, "there's no gimmick anymore."

That's the problem when we play around with style. It's easy to use grammar tricks to make things "different," but as so often happens, the results are long on technique and short on substance. You may admire your inventiveness, but the reader is left to ponder the sense of it. It's far better to develop style through word usage than to reach for grammar tricks. The urge to uncover that "personal voice" is powerful indeed, and you should guard against the urge overcoming basic good sense when you produce your work. Be suspicious of an inclination to get tricky and jazzy with style; be especially suspicious when exotic grammar is used ...

Blunder No. 12

Such as … long blank spaces between paragraphs or between dialogue passages … varied paragraph indents (such as my student's narrative tale) … strange punctuation known mainly to the author (see Chapter 2) … a phalanx of exclamation points (turning emphasis into pretentious posturing) … an oversupply of ellipses (breaking the story into uncontrollable fragments) … repeating the same word over and over, line after line …

Cause and effect are the golden rule here. To develop style and a "personal voice," you have to be clear on *why* you use what you use. Sometimes you can fool yourself quite easily.

A few years ago I co-authored a nonfiction book that was going to dramatize a series of events. We were going to quote from actual interviews, but we also would re-create dialogue, providing we could establish its authenticity. Our purpose was to get away from a straight reportorial style and to utilize fiction-writing technique. But we were concerned about some of the dialogue because we figured the reader might assume it to be a truthful rendering instead of a re-creation. So we put the following note at the beginning of the book:

> For purposes of this book we have avoided the use of quotation marks because the settings of particular dialogue and stories may have changed … However, where a dash (—) is used, the words and circumstances, with minor editing for clarity, are actual … Where dialogue appears without being set off by a dash, the words and circumstances have been reconstructed …

Then we sat back and patted ourselves on the shoulders. We'd played fair with the reader, and we'd used an imaginative approach to style and punctuation. Dialogue passages would either be set off with a dash or nothing at all, depending upon the source of the quote. We'd preserved dramatic effect.

Ah, we thought we were so clever! It would be our "personal voice," an innovative, sculptured style.

But few raves came our way. Instead, we found ourselves criticized for overcomplicating the storytelling apparatus. Readers didn't want to keep a guide at their elbow, noting whether *this* dialogue passage reproduces what was actually said or whether it's only a re-creation offered by the authors.

In other words, we committed the most egregious blunder a writer can commit: we interrupted the story by giving out stage directions. Readers who have to be oriented every few lines quickly become disenchanted, and their attentions will turn elsewhere.

We had become so tricky and jazzy that to those who really counted—our readers—we'd provided confusion and disarray. The grammar might have been creative, but few were willing to accept it as an exciting new way to tell a story.

And we paid the ultimate price: lukewarm reviews and modest sales. It was a lesson I've never forgotten.

13

DON'T ADD ADVERBS AND ADJECTIVES TO PRETTIFY YOUR PROSE

Some years ago the fine short story writer Raymond Carver offered recollections about learning to write from teacher and novelist John Gardner. "I remember him as being very patient," Carver wrote in *Fires*, "wanting me to understand what he was trying to show me, telling me over and over how important it was to have the right words saying what I wanted them to say. Nothing vague or blurred, no smoky-glass prose ... He made me see that absolutely everything was important in a short story. It was of consequence where the commas and periods went."

This attention to detail is precisely why Raymond Carver acquired a reputation as a short story master; rarely, if ever, was a word or a series of words purposeless and uncertain. His prose was tight and emphatic, and his phrases never dangled or were superfluous. His craftsmanship honed his work to its essence.

There aren't many Raymond Carvers in this world, but each of us can learn some important things from the way he approached his writing. Sentence structure and punctuation were crucial, the proper word was essential, and what was omitted as important as what was inserted.

Which brings us to adverbs and adjectives. Clearly, Carver would cast a suspicious eye on these forms of speech because many times they add little to what is already on the page. Frequently, they are not important, and in a short story, that means they have no business there.

Many inexperienced writers throw in "pretty" words to make their prose more dramatic and meaningful. But such cosmetic touch-up often turns out to be redundant or simply uninspiring. Take adverbs such as "lovingly" or "speedily" or "haltingly." They each point to some circumstance or emotion or movement, yet do they offer solid impact?

He whispered to her *lovingly* ...

She zoomed around the oval *speedily* ...

He stuttered *haltingly* ...

In the last two instances, the verbs themselves provide the acting and the emotion in the sentences; the adverbs merely underscore what the verb has already described. Is it possible to "zoom" without doing so speedily ... or to "stutter" without doing it in halting fashion? These are redundancies, and they do little for the prose except to give it an awkward cast.

The stone sank *quickly* ...

The fire truck bell clanged *loudly*...

How else would a stone sink but quickly? How else would a fire truck bell clang but loudly? The key is to gauge the relationship of the adverb and the verb it modifies: Are they saying essentially the same thing? If so, there is a redundancy, and the adverb should come out—fast!

It isn't only redundancies that adverbs can generate. They also encourage lazy writing. Take the earlier example, "he whispered to her lovingly ..." I suppose he could whisper many things, including words, which are loving, but somehow the adverbial tail seems a lazy way out. By using "lovingly" the writer is really—and we've heard this before—*telling* instead of showing. Far more dramatic would be to write:

> He whispered words of love … *my sweet*, *dear lover*, *my angel* … he purred his contentment, his joy …

No adverb here, and the drama is enhanced. I've shown those things that he whispered lovingly, and the reader has to be more involved in the story.

It has become a cliché to use the adverbial tail time and time again. In addition to minimizing the dramatic effect of the action, it grinds on the reader's ear (remember, readers "hear" as well as read). All those words ending in "-ly," not doing much for the sentence, not creating much of a word picture … Who could blame readers for wondering why the words were there in the first place?

And who could blame these same readers for laying the book aside? "Most adverbs," says William Zinsser, "are unnecessary." He's right. And when it's important to prettify your prose, there are better ways to do it.

Not with adjectives, though. These suffer the same general malady as adverbs—usually they are too numerous, they clutter up our writing, and they can turn a deft phrase into a ponderous mass. Consider:

> The house had an empty feeling to it, the air stale with undefined kitchen odors …

This is a tight, dramatic description. But what happens when I add more adjectives to "prettify" it?

> The dark, dreary house had an empty, suspicious feel to it, the thick air stale and sour with undefined, scary kitchen odors …

Do all these adjectives add much at all? An empty house implies something strange and sinister, so do I need "suspicious"? Do I also need "dark, dreary"? An empty house might be these things as well, but I'm not unmindful that a sinister house may also be bright and sunlit (though it does stretch my credibility

Blunder No. 13

83

a bit). At least, though, I should dispense with one of the two adjectives, either "dark" or "dreary" because taken together, they are a well-recognized cliché ... and they almost mean the same thing.

But note the other bits of overwriting: if the air were stale, wouldn't it also be thick? And wouldn't it be sour, as well?

Mark Twain had it right: "As to the Adjective: when in doubt, strike it out." The tendency is to try and beef up the noun being modified. It's human, I suppose; most of us can never be *that* sure we're getting our point across. Decorate that noun some more, your fragile self-confidence hears. Don't run the risk the prose will fall flat because it isn't distinctive enough.

Ah ... you think, a little word or two, here and there ... it'll catch the reader's attention, it'll keep her reading ...

Well, yes and no. Yes, it might certainly catch the reader's attention, but never underestimate the kind of attention that could be. Try *negative* attention, the kind that might push the reader away from the prose. Consider:

He was cheered by the *friendly* smiles ...

He spied a group of *dirty* street-urchins ...

Do the adjectives "friendly" and "dirty" add anything to the sentences? Read the words without adjectives ... Now read them with the adjectives inserted. Is anything more provided by including the adjectives? They contain the thought that's already in the noun they modify, so they aren't doing anything for the sentences except taking up space. Aren't smiles usually "friendly"? Aren't street-urchins usually "dirty"? Why the adjectives, then?

The short answer is that you're trying to prettify your prose, to give it a lushness that will settle on the reader. Adjectives are a way of lengthening your sentences and providing a more complicated word picture, and this, in turn, will intrigue the reader

because there will seem to be substance in the prose. The reader will experience more, and hence, the reader will enjoy it more.

But misplaced adjectives can do as much damage as botched-up syntax. If the adjectives are there only to prettify the prose, they should be eliminated. The key is, adjectives should be used only when they highlight something the noun can't highlight. For example:

He slipped into the *darkened* alley...

Not all alleys are dark, so now you know this one will be. But suppose this had read:

He slipped into the *narrow* alley...

Alleys are usually narrow (if they aren't narrow, they're called streets or roads), so the adjective isn't telling any more than is offered by the noun. This is "prettifying" the prose, and it isn't pretty at all. Reach for adjectives that give more information than can already be found in the noun—when, in fact, an adjective should be used at all. Frankly, most adjectives are not needed. What benefits they offer are usually much less than the havoc they create.

Some years ago, a wise man (with perhaps a sexist bent) said, "pick adjectives the way you would diamonds or a mistress..."

Carefully, he meant, so carefully.

14

DON'T SPRINKLE THE POET'S URGE OVER THE NARRATOR'S PRODUCT

Herman Melville once wrote, after describing Ahab's eyes "glowing like coals" with a "splintered helmet of a brow ...":

> Oh, immortal infancy, and innocency of the azure! Invisible winged creatures that frolic around us! Sweet childhood of air and sky! how oblivious were ye of old Ahab's close-coiled woe!

In four or five paragraphs Melville could develop his symbolism and his imagery with magnificent phrases such as "Aloft, like a royal czar and king, the sun seemed giving this gentle air to the bold and rolling sea ..." and "That glad, happy air, that winsome sky, did at last stroke and caress him ..."

This, of course, is poetry in narrative form, and many writers have been lulled into belief that such writing is the only pinnacle to strive for, that poetic flair woven into fiction will make it more "literary."

The truth is ... it could accomplish the opposite. Squeezing in poetic touches may push clear, direct prose to awkward, cumbersome results. Style is not so easily manipulated, and the poet's effect is not so easily developed.

But we see Melville's grand images, or in more contemporary terms, those of John Updike or Philip Roth or Toni Morrison, and some writers believe that here must lie the path to success. It is "good writing," it is "literary writing," and they tend to see it as the one true style.

It isn't, of course. This so-called "high style" of writing is quite rare, and in today's world of quickened expectations and instant results, it often doesn't work. What Melville could accomplish with images such as "Sweet childhood of air and sky" and "bold and rolling sea" might even be ponderous and overwritten if found in a modern novel. Phrasing and grammatical effects that might work with the "high style," such as pages-long paragraphs, endless sentences, and poetic touches like internal rhyming and alliteration, are difficult to control. If they don't flow from the writer's mind to the page, they become awkward and ill fitting.

Suppose you wanted to describe the flight of sea birds across the breaking waves. You could write:

> ... their wings whispered wondrously while wavelets whooshed their watery way ...

Or you could write:

> ... the large birds glided above the foam, searching the swirl for unwary prey ...

The more direct approach is certainly preferable because it describes something that is happening, instead of something that the writer hopes the reader will feel. That's not to say you shouldn't attempt to spark feelings in the reader, only that doing so is a delicate act. You run a tremendous risk when you try to write in the "high style"; it demands so much from you and the standards by which you are judged remain uncompromising.

I have a friend who has been struggling to produce top-shelf literature for several decades; he is what many call a "purist" in that he does not wish to write solely to be published. Each day he follows a writing schedule that includes a minimum of six hours at his computer, and he believes that eventually he will produce a fine, literary American novel.

He hasn't done that yet, however. He has published several short stories—always in the "little" magazines—and he has also produced the occasional "literary" nonfiction piece.

But no novel. One day I asked him if he was discouraged.

"Sometimes," he admitted, "but that's the price I have to pay."

"Why not lower your sights?" I suggested.

He gave me a bleak smile. "I write literature. Everything else is manufactured."

"Define 'literature' for me."

"It's the best writing you can do. It proceeds on two or three levels, it's filled with poetic flair and imagery, it takes the reader to places the reader would never hope to reach without the writer's guidance. It deals with eternal truths."

I mentioned a couple of currently popular mystery writers whose work seemed to transcend their genre.

"Manufactured prose," he said. "Not literature."

This is a man consumed with writing the "high style" so much so that he has put himself adrift in a sea of frustration. Perhaps he'll achieve his goal eventually, but after those decades of purist struggle, it's hard to imagine anything satisfying him.

One of the dangers of seeking to write "poetically" is the failure to appreciate the thin line between poetic effect and pseudo-poetic effect. Where Melville can write about "bold and rolling sea," the inexperienced writer might produce "dangerous and bouncy sea" or "sweaty, suffering sea."

Look at what the inexperienced writer produces: "dangerous and bouncy sea …" Can a realistic portrait be made from this? What's the effect on the reader? "Dangerous" may certainly be the consequence of "bold and rolling sea," but as a descriptive adjective, it doesn't show us much. "Frothy" or "thunderous" or "mountainous" give a more dramatic picture, and of course they also make us aware that the sea is dangerous.

Blunder No. 14

89

Look, also, at the juxtaposition of "dangerous" and "bouncy"; is there poetry here? Do these words create images as profound as "bold and rolling"? Is there any majesty in a sea that is "bouncy"? "Dangerous" is a word with more character, but when it is used with "bouncy," it loses some force. When you take the two together, you find a clash of sounds and a clash of imagery—the words just don't fit well together.

From the inexperienced writer's point of view, the description might seem apt; a "dangerous and bouncy" sea might well exist. But when that imagery is translated on the page, what's factual and what's poetic are simply not the same.

Look at "sweaty, suffering sea ..." There's a modest attempt at alliteration, but note the clash in poetic effect. Does the sea sweat? Can it be personified to the extent that it appears to sweat? And how does the sea suffer? Usually, it's people *on the sea* who suffer. Though Melville wrote of the majesty of the sea and its power, not all writers might see it this way. There can be a devilish flavor to the sea, perhaps a betraying or vindictive character, even a solemn and benign effect.

But "sweaty and suffering"? Hardly.

And it's bad poetry, too, because the words don't work smoothly, in spite of the attempt at alliteration. The word meanings are not a good fit, they don't flow, one to the other, like "bold and rolling." It's as if two boards were butted against one another, and the tongues and grooves were of different sizes. Grammatically, what's happening is a syntax deviation where word meanings and sentence structure are manipulated to achieve a result that doesn't occur. If you strive to embrace the poetic touch, then you'd better be confident you understand what it means.

Because if you fail, the glitches in your writing will stand out for all to see.

Understand there is nothing wrong with following the "high style," and that in proper hands it will produce memorable prose.

But then understand that few writers have the talent to produce such writing, and that slavish perseverance might bring about a lifetime of bare results—similar to my friend who chases the grail of "literary prose." Much better to develop a more realistic attitude. There's only one John Updike, only one Toni Morrison, only Philip Roth ... but there are many ways to write and many styles to follow.

Simple, direct prose may be best. The "bold and rolling sea" could be the "storm-tossed sea" or "the gray, ominous sea." You needn't stretch to achieve some unique poetic application. That highly evocative Melville line: "Oh, immortal infancy, and innocency of the azure," which refers to the purity and permanence of the heavens, could read, "the sky was a radiant blue, undisturbed and solid." Not as poetic, certainly, but the idea comes through.

You want to avoid working so hard to achieve the poetic touch that you produce a self-conscious effect ... something so awkward it calls attention to your technique. Strange, exotic grammar will do this, as will phrases and words that step away from the general style.

Perhaps the best approach about using the poetic touch is to remember Robert Frost's reputed response to a young writer he encountered at a writer's conference.

"What writing do you do?" Frost is supposed to have asked.

"Oh, I'm a poet," the young man said, beaming.

"No," Frost remarked, "you may write verse, but the world will tell you when you are a poet."

The reality shouldn't be overlooked. Not all of us are—or need to be—poets.

But there's still plenty of writing to do.

15

DON'T LET RHYTHM AND SOUND TURN SOUR

"Think of grammar the way an orchestra leader uses his percussion section," a writing teacher might say to his students. "The beat has to be there, otherwise the music has nothing to work against. It has no rhythm."

In effect, the percussionists become punctuation and syntax for the orchestra.

Remember, readers "hear" as well as read the written word. Writers have to understand that clunkish rhythms and sounds will turn the reader off. The percussionist in an orchestra provides a floor that allows the other musicians to develop their artistry. But if the floor isn't there, the musical artistry collapses.

So it is with punctuation and syntax: They develop the *floor* that allows rhythmic, sweet-sounding prose to develop.

Consider this:

> I knew the jalopy had poor tires, though it had a powerful engine, but there wasn't much time to spare because all the apple crates would be gone, and we knew who would have them, and then it would be too late ...

One long sentence where the point of view changes from first person ("I") to first person plural ("we"). The syntax is rough, and the grammar has no rhythm. It's one long mishmash of clashing sounds.

Now, consider this:

> The jalopy had poor tires maybe, but it had a powerful engine ... those apple crates would be gone if we didn't get over there ... no time to spare ... he'd get them ... him! ...

The syntax and grammar *do something* in this second instance; they establish tension and drama, and they produce a rhythmic touch. Note that each sentence or clause is shorter than the one preceding it, that the syntax doesn't flip between points of view, that the punctuation (the ellipses) provide a natural bridge between the clauses, and that the prose seems to flow. There's a rhythm here, and the reader becomes part of the work, sensing the movement and figuratively keeping time.

Maintaining rhythm with punctuation and syntax is not hard if you're aware how it can influence what the reader takes in. The point is to know it has an effect, then you can always do something to develop it. Simple commas, for example, can create staccato rhythm if they are used with a series of single words or short phrases ... or they can slow things down if breaks in a long sentence are needed. Deliberately jumping from first person to third person and back again within the same paragraph, over and over, depicts rhythmic confusion while locking onto first person *or* third person (second person, too) and not deviating, page after page, provides rhythmic effect. It's the rhythm of the metronome, and most jazz musicians will acknowledge that their music has to have the percussionist beating that rhythm, same beat same sound, over and over and over ... for the artistry in the other musicians to flower.

In the hands of a master storyteller, the rhythmic character of punctuation and syntax can be portrayed so well. Here's Thomas Wolfe from his book *Of Time and the River*, and he has Helen Gant, the daughter of the dying Eugene Gant, attempting to understand why a group of blue collar men have come to the house to pay respects to her father. Wolfe reveals her thoughts as she approaches the group:

"Why-why-why—these men are really the closest friends he's got—not rich men like Uncle Will or Uncle Jim or even Mr. Sluder—but men like Mike Fogarty—and Jannadeau—and Mr. Duncan—and Alec Ramsey—and Ernest Pegram—and Ollie Gant—but—but good heavens no!" she thought, almost desperately—"surely these are not his closest friends—why-why—of course, they're decent people—they're honest men—but they're only common people—I've always considered them as just *working* men—and-and-and—my God!" she thought, with that terrible feeling of discovery we have when we suddenly see ourselves as others see us—"do you suppose that's the way people in this town think of Papa?..."

Note the rhythmic flow here, the way Wolfe uses dashes to separate clauses, and the fact that most of the clauses are not complete sentences. The dashes set the rhythm of the paragraph, speed up the action, and give the prose an immediacy that grabs the reader and insists the reader pay attention. Read this aloud; note how the choppy phrases form a steady rhythm and how you can hear her thinking as she moves towards the men. The rhythm is so strong that you're not put off when Wolfe breaks it momentarily to offer an aside about seeing ourselves as others see us. But then he picks up the rhythm of her inner thought again.

Word-sounds are as important as prose rhythms. Suppose, for example, you wanted to describe a poor but dignified-looking elderly woman, and you were trying to establish her respectability. Would you write about her "solid, stiff carriage adorned with ratty clothes...."?

Or would we refer to her "smooth, sculpted face, fine-boned figure and sturdy stride, her ripped, ill-fitting housecoat...."?

In the first phrase, the word-sounds don't work well because they are jerky, they bump against each other. "Solid, stiff..." is alliterative and doesn't cause you to cringe when you say it, but when you add the second part, "...adorned with ratty clothes..." the word-sounds are dissonant, they aren't pleasing to the ear, and that's not the effect you want (obviously, if you want to create

dissonant sounds in order to establish a mood of conflict or chaos or general disarray, this would work well). The result is that what you hoped would be an admirable portrait of an elderly woman becomes ragged and less effective.

The second phrase is better because the alliteration is carried further (three clauses instead of one) and because the description of her poverty is not as harsh as writing "…adorned with ratty clothes…." There is empathy in the description of the housecoat as "ripped, ill-fitting…." There is no empathy in using "ratty" for her clothes.

The same type of approach works with punctuation. You can use marks such as the dash (—) to convey rapid thought or action, or the ellipsis (…) to convey heightening suspense or a pause between movement, and the word-sounds take on different effects (see Chapter 9). Consider:

> there—there! —a face—no, no, a white light—hurry—no time, it *is* a face—I'm falling…

And this:

> there … there! … a face … no, no a white light … hurry … no time … it *is* a face … I'm falling…

In the first example, everything is speeded up because of the dash, but with the second example, the ellipses slow the action down a bit, allowing a deeper effect on the reader. The word-sounds coming into the reader's mind convey the speed-up or slow-down the writer wishes to portray, and the story's effect will be influenced. The same consequence occurs no matter what the punctuation; commas, semicolons, exclamation points, single or double quotation marks, they all add something to the "sounds" that blossom from the written page.

And writers should understand that the right words producing the wrong sound is no different than playing *Rhapsody in Blue* on the piccolo.

In the hands of a good writer, word-sounds from a variety of sources can develop their own personality. See how John T. Lescroart, using syntax and punctuation, develops excitement and unreality in this passage from his suspense novel, *Dead Irish*. Alphonse and Linda have suddenly come upon a huge cache of money after they've broken into an office safe:

> He crossed back to the desk. The packet of money fit easily into the front pocket of the camouflage pants. "Goddamn," he said, surprised at the high end of his voice. He turned to look at Linda, still kneeling by the safe. "God-damn! You hear me? God ... god-damn."
>
> He felt like he had to go to the bathroom. "How much is there?" Linda asked, her voice small now behind the cavernous roaring rush in Alphonse's ears... .

The author uses both description and dialogue to get out the word-sounds, and the results are finely tuned. Note the punctuation: "Goddamn" is a whole word, but the next time it's used it's "God-damn" with a dash ... and then the next time another dash, after an ellipsis.

Can't you hear Alphonse utter his astonishment? Don't the words come at you via their sounds? But the author goes a step further and describes Alphonse's state of mind, having him use the "high end of his voice," and causing him to have to go to the bathroom and hearing a "cavernous roaring rush" in his ears. In syntax terms, all of these words and phrases flow smoothly because they fit together well; there isn't a word-sound sticking its clunky notes into the music. For example, read aloud the phrase, "cavernous roaring rush ...." It sounds exactly like what it's supposed to mean, a huge spillage of sound, deep and overwhelming.

This is the way to sing a sweet tune with rhythm and sound. Careful attention to how words fit makes sour notes into beautiful melody.

16

DON'T DABBLE WITH "SMOKY" WORDS

I took a writing course in college from a wise old teacher whose number of publications I could never hope to duplicate. His manner was gentle but his standards were exacting. Students soon came to understand there were certain writing habits they should avoid because his negative comments would bite and bite deeply.

One of these was the use of what he called "airy" words. With his ruddy complexion and pursed mouth, he would listen passively as a student read her work aloud ... until a word or phrase caught his attention.

Then, he would shake his head sadly, waving the student to silence. "Smoke rings," he would utter, "nothing there."

We realized his criticism forced us to weigh words more carefully, to consider alternatives and to concentrate on tightening our prose. "Smoke rings!" came to be generic for writing criticism, and the use of the term carried its own cachet—only students who had taken a class with this writing teacher felt qualified to utter it.

We used to discuss what words should be singled out.

"*Beautiful*?" someone might suggest.

"Smoke rings," would come the response.

"I know what's beautiful, everyone does."

"But can we feel it or smell it?"

"*Hopefully*?" another might suggest. "No doubt about that."

We would have a good laugh. Everyone knew *that* adverb wasn't good for much of anything.

"How about *very*?" I remember asking. I had a special reason because earlier that day I had turned in a manuscript, which read:

It had been a difficult climb, a *very* difficult climb, and now he was exhausted...

"Smoke rings," the writing teacher had said. "It adds nothing. A 'difficult climb' is sufficient."

"I was looking for emphasis," I had said.

"It's in the word already."

Now my classmates and I debated the use of "very." Finally someone said, "Anyone notice it's usually attached to a strong word: 'very hard'...' very strong'...'very heavy'...?" Take away "very," we saw, and the adjective it modifies stands straight and true. How much better off can one be if one is "strong" or "very strong"? How much more uncomfortable would it be if something is "heavy" instead of "very heavy"? How much more durable would something be if it is "hard" or "very hard"?

The truth is there are certain words or groups of words that add nothing to anyone's prose and are better left in the word barn. On the surface, they offer a pleasing step to greater emphasis or more specificity. But they are an illusion. The savvy writer can sense that they accomplish little except to clutter up the prose, and their presence in the sentence has a way of diluting the impact of all the other words and phrases.

Such a word is "just"...as in "Just wait a moment" or "He's just kidding." Read these two phrases aloud as written and then read them aloud without the "just." Does this simple four-letter word add anything at all? On the contrary, it probably takes some of the immediacy from the phrases. "Wait a moment" is clear and direct—it's an unqualified imperative. "He's kidding" is an undiluted explanation, yet when "just" is inserted, both phrases become less effective, more querulous in the first example, more excuse-oriented in the second example. "Just" tends to soil the clarity that's in the more direct phrasing, and one thing above all must guide the serious writer: Write what you mean and mean what you write.

"Just" makes it hard to do. It has little purpose in a sentence, other than as a colloquial expression from the mouth of a character who is portrayed in this manner: "Just right, sir ... I'll just be a moment ... Just now ..." And if we look carefully, we can see that the meaning of each phrase is carried, not by the use of "just," but by the other words. "Right, sir ... I'll be a moment ... now ..."

Smoke rings.

Some people, however, are not so casually convinced. Once I had a student who couldn't understand why words such as "very" and "just" should be wiped off the written page. "After all," she said, "these are the words we use in conversation."

I had to agree with her as far as that went. But then, of course, our conversation is often dotted with ill-fitting grammar because we are speaking in what amounts to a first draft, while our writing can be edited and re-edited until it sails along smoothly. But that really wasn't the point. I knew what that student had missed, and it was a distinction that many inexperienced writers fail to see.

"Conversation is ... well, conversation," I said. "But what we write is more than that. It's conversation or narrative ... *with drama*! (See Chapter 6.) We try to tell a story, and in doing that, we have to develop the dramatic effects of what is either said or done. Sometimes that drama tends to get lost in real life, but as writers we aren't allowed to let that happen."

I went on to explain that it was true we use "smoky" words in our speech and conversation, even in our thoughts. But when you sit down to write and you know there will be readers who want to be entertained, then good writing demands you think of drama before you think of what happens in true life.

You have to be careful with smoky words, however, because sometimes they can change skins and become more important and

more useful. One of these is a word that dangles with pretensions: "rather," as in "The church is really rather far ..."

Now, there's a combination that really says nothing ("really" is another "smoky" word, as well as a shoulder-cringing colloquialism). Remove "rather" and we have "The church is really far ..." which makes sense and stands up well.

Yet there are those who find something elegant in the use of "rather" as a qualifier or modifier. The same people, no doubt, who answer a question "somewhat" directly or who turn up their nose at one who is "a touch" overdressed or a "tad" uncertain. These are writers for whom a blurred vision offers safety because they need not display themselves, warts and all. They hold something back, and in the process they turn their writing to mush.

Or take "really." It suffers from the same smokiness as "rather." As a qualifier or modifier, it is also superfluous. Substitute it for "rather," as in, "really/rather overdressed" or "really/rather uncertain," then remove both and read them again. Nothing—not an ounce of sense—is lost.

Or, perhaps think of it this way:

I'd rather not have really,
And I really don't want rather,
For no matter how I use them,
It makes me want to lose them.

There is one aspect of "rather" you shouldn't overlook, though. It can serve a purpose as a mood changer instead of a modifier, similar to "however" or "meanwhile" or "nevertheless." And when it's used this way, it loses its "smoky" connotation: "Rather than give in, I decided to fight to the finish ..." It changes the direction of the prose from the preceding sentence, providing a new tempo or different characterization. It is useful and, therefore, perfectly appropriate.

Rather we took the left fork…

Rather you than me…

There are other qualifiers that add smoke to our phrasing: "a bit" and "kind of," to name two. The important thing to note is that when you write, "I'd like a bit more please," you're not adding substance to the prose, and this effect is the same with most of the qualifiers. Is there a solid difference between "I'd like more please" and the same phrase with "a bit" inserted? Or if you write, "He went kind of far," are you adding anything by using the qualifier? Doesn't "he went far" sound cleaner and neater? How about "quite" or "sort of" or "possibly"? Is there a difference?

"Smoky" words have allure, no doubt. They *seem* so useful, but when you reach out to grasp them, there's nothing there.

Really.

17

DON'T EXPECT THE MAID (EDITOR, THAT IS) TO CLEAN UP YOUR MESS

There! You place the final period of the final sentence of the final paragraph. It's done, a complete story. You weren't sure you'd ever get this far, but you persisted; now you can pat yourself on the back. And it's a good feeling.

Of course, you know you have some editing, but there's time for that. Relish the moment of completion for now. Doing the story is the important thing. You have *that* over with.

Don't be fooled, though. The story is sill incomplete; you are certainly *not* finished. That nugget of literary gold you have mined needs molding and polishing; it needs *preparation* before it can be offered to a publisher, then to the public.

A myth many inexperienced writers share is that editors will "fix-up" the grammar in a manuscript to allow the irresistible story to shine through. The demands of grammar, it is thought, are of secondary importance, and any competent editor can do what's necessary to tidy things up.

Perhaps we remember too well those intriguing tales of Thomas Wolfe dropping thousands of blotted, marked-up pages on Maxwell Perkins (which resulted in *Look Homeward, Angel*) or Jack Kerouac walking in on Bennett Cerf and handing him a massive teletype roll on which he'd scrawled a story (which resulted in *On the Road*). But these are vivid exceptions because in both cases the writers had taken their work as far as they humanly could. Their "mess" certainly needed straightening out, but they were not able to do it without help.

That's a giant step from where most of us are. The "mess" you make, by and large, you can—and should—straighten out yourself. Sure, it would be dandy to spin out a story and let someone else pick up the grammar after you. It's an elegant approach to the writer's trade. But it's not realistic, and it's not going to fill you with true accomplishment. Most of us have a working familiarity with punctuation, style, and language use (if you don't, you better look for another profession), and we know what the general rules are (that doesn't mean you may not want to break them; see Chapter 29). Why, then, would you not prefer to stay in charge of your own material? If it's within your power to clean up your own mess, why not have pride of authorship and simply *do it*?

One day I received a call from a man in Hollywood who had read one of my books. He was intrigued by the way I wrote and what I wrote about. He had spent years in the movie business and now he wanted to do something more "literary." He had written a number of stories, and he asked me to take a look at a few and suggest a publisher.

"They need some minor editing," he said, "not much, really." When they arrived, it took only a few moments to realize he wanted me to "clean up his mess." The paper was fresh, the printouts were neat, but the stories were overwritten, poorly punctuated and loaded with clichés. Some were pointless, others awkwardly conceived. It was as if he had taken a handful of words and thrown them on the page.

He called me a few days later for a reaction. When I told him the stories had little chance to be published, he was unfazed. "That's okay," he said, "I've got hundreds more. I never rewrite, you know. First draft, that's all I ever do. I can't stand to rewrite."

He missed the point. Rewriting isn't bitter medicine—it's professional awareness. It's a sign of supreme naïveté, rank amateurism, and unfettered arrogance to assume any piece of work can't or shouldn't be rewritten. Joseph Conrad was reputed to

have said that it took him an entire morning to insert a single adverb...and an entire afternoon to remove it. That's true professionalism, and that's what my friend from Hollywood failed to grasp. If the object of writing is to get your best effort published, then you should be willing to offer the most professional piece of work for consideration.

Because—and some writers tend to forget this—editors are professionals, too. They make their living out of words and books (just as we do), and they expect to give and receive professional treatment. If you submit something that's in obvious need of grammar tune-up (such as a pile of overdone clichés or a paucity of proper punctuation), the editor will sigh and send a rejection slip—probably without a personal note. Most editors recognize amateurism within a few pages, and their patience is not unlimited.

Then, too, cleaning up a writer's mess takes time, and editors would rather devote their limited hours to manuscripts that offer a smoother, more rewarding path to completion. That doesn't mean that editors can't spot a nugget of good literature inside the most chaotic morass, only that you improve your chances of getting the editor's attention if you clean up your own mess *before* sending the manuscript.

The answer lies in attitude—especially yours. In my writing classes one of my first requirements is that every submitted manuscript must be typed or printed out. I don't do this because I relish torture, nor am I on the outs with handwriting. What I'm trying to do is get my students to *care* about the form of their submissions. The more formal I require them to be, the more serious their attitude will be, and the more careful they will be about what they turn in.

It means they will rewrite, which will modify their "mess," and it means that I will be able to read clean copy (believe me, this is a distinct benefit!). The ultimate purpose is to have all of them understand the need to produce their best work. Then if there's still a mess, I have no problem helping to clean it up.

Blunder No. 17

DON'T HUG FAD WORDS WITHOUT YOUR FINGERS CROSSED

There's little doubt we have a penchant for trends, and this is especially true with words or expressions. Something new—anything different—and our antennae quiver. It isn't because the settled side of our language is dull or ineffective; on the contrary, the English language may be the lushest language of all (for more on this, see Chapter 28), and it's not uncommon to have two, three, even four separate words or phrases meaning the same thing applied to a particular item.

But our language is organic, in the sense that it is alive, always growing, always changing. This irrepressibility is what's intriguing, and when we first hear or read a word or phrase that explodes with novelty, we're like the child at a toy store ... *we've got to have it*!

Only, in our case, it means we've got to use it, somewhere, somehow in conversation ... or sometimes, unfortunately, in our writing.

I say "unfortunately" because a novelty only retains its freshness so long as it remains a novelty. Look at what was trendy or novel fifty to sixty years ago: *Kilroy was here! ... hey-bop-a-re-bop ...solid!*

Where have they gone today? Would you ever see graffiti announcing "Kilroy was here!"... or that a person's accomplishment was "solid" won? Yet all those years ago words and phrases like these were in common usage—they appeared in newspapers, magazines, and books with regularity. Few writers felt the need to explain what they meant by calling something "solid" or the significance of a wall or bench containing the phrase "Kilroy was

here!" These were trendy words and expressions, and if the writer understood them, he could be sure the readers would, too.

The savvy writer, however, would see things differently. True, these words and phrases had a comfortable, acknowledged currency, and the writer could use them without wondering if the readers might be baffled. But wasn't there also another side to consider?

What if these trendy words and phrases were not so useful as first thought? What if they tended to date material and make it obsolete? What if they tended to disappear from the language as quickly as they entered it?

The proof is before us. How many trendy expressions from the 1940s and 1950s survive today? Who remembers going on a "motor trip" ... or wanting to practice "vamping" ... or hating the "truant officer"? Suppose you insert words or phrases like this into your modern prose. What's the probable reaction?

"Huh?"

"That's the way my grandparents talked."

"When was this stuff written?"

Whenever you're tempted to weave something that smacks of faddishness in your prose, ask yourself: *Where will it be ten years from now?* That's all it takes, ten years or less, and most words and phrases that rode in on a fad will ride out again. They'll disappear into historical dictionaries and academic study, but they will not carve out a permanent place in your writer's inventory.

You needn't look back far to get a good look at the way fad words come and go. Stretch back to the 1960s and early 1970s, that glorious time that held so much promise and left us gasping with uncertainty. "The times they are a-changin'..." sang Bob Dylan, and that was certainly true. Some of the biggest changes happened to language, and we saw a flood of new words and phrases spread through our common, everyday usage:

"Let's split this scene ..."

"Here comes the fuzz ..."

"He's tripping on acid ..."

We talked of something "not being my bag" ... or of "flower power" ... or of someone "not being wrapped too tight." These were words and phrases of a dynamic time, and writers could be forgiven for believing they had permanence because the times themselves were so special. But the experienced writer was not so taken in. Fad words were still fad words, and by the time the 1970s had gone, people no longer spoke (or wrote) of "splitting a scene." By then there were new fad words joining the language, and writers who stuck with the old found themselves as dated as if they written of "motor trips" and "hey-bop-a-re-bop."

This all comes down to a matter of style. When you use fad words that have lost their faddishness, you come face to face with syntax, which, in turn, means grammar. A word improperly used—whether it's misspelled, saddled with a wrong connotation, or simply old-fashioned—is a blemish to acceptable writing, and it will affect the reader's enjoyment and ultimate reaction.

The experienced writer produces good work through *general style*, not through an occasional fad word or phrase. When you read John Updike, for instance, or Joan Didion, you are struck by the inherent elegance in their prose, and if you look closely, you see nothing resembling fad words or phrases. They recognize that it doesn't take much to date a writer's expressions, that within a couple of years, sometimes, a writer's work could be obsolete, especially if fad words and phrases are part of the mix. They may have characters speak in the jargon of their time to give relevance and immediacy, but that's an exception to the rule. Characters in the 1960s did speak of "splitting a scene," characters in the 1940s did speak of "snafus," but such fad words and phrases were used

sparingly, at most. And when the authors spoke to the reader, fad words and phrases disappeared.

Yet fad words and phrases pop up every year, decade after decade. The savvy writer knows how to watch for them creeping into his prose. We're in a new century now, and within a few years we'll wonder whatever happened to … "I'm outta here!" … "chill out!" … "awesome!" … "nerd."

The savvy writer will remember, though. Not because such words and phrases were incisive or poetic, because they weren't.

He will remember them because they should be avoided.

19

DON'T GET CUTE WITH SPELLINGS AND DIALOGUE

"Dere Barbara," I wrote one day when I was sixteen. "I think of u most of the time, espeshully during skool. The tichers ask me about u, and I say u don't rite much, so it's hard to b sure u like boarding school. In jim during the mid-weak brake, I called 2 tichers by 1st names, they didn't laugh."

I thought I was being clever, and I thought Barbara would be impressed. It was the first letter I'd written to her, and I wanted to make it something she wouldn't forget. I knew she would be meeting new people, and teachers had been telling me for quite a while I could write well, so I thought I'd show off ... and remind her I was around.

My letter went on for four pages in the style above, and I pictured blonde, blue-eyed Barbara smiling as she read my words, then brushing away light tears of remembrance, then running to tell her friends about the "neat" letter she had received.

It never happened that way, of course. Blonde-blue-eyed Barbara delivered the clearest answer I could have received.

She never wrote back. Not a single word of response. Nothing.

I saw her when she came home for vacation, and it was obvious her feelings for me were passive, at best. "What did you think of my letter?" I finally had the courage to ask.

Her brow knitted briefly. "Oh, that." She shrugged. "I thought you were making fun of me."

"I wanted to write something different," I said.

"Why?"

It's a question we writers should always ask ourselves when we're tempted to fool around with spellings and word sounds. Certainly there's a challenge in developing a form of newspeak (or new-write, to be completely accurate), and most writers like the fact they may produce words or phrases no one else has come up with. It's a feather in our creative cap ... but it may well be that the feather comes made of lead.

Barbara thought I was making fun of her when my purpose was exactly the opposite. She couldn't understand my deliberate misspellings because she couldn't see their purpose. Think of Barbara as the reader out there, that shady force you seek to impress, and then imagine that Barbara's reaction to my cute spelling and grammar would not be different from any reader's reaction to the same thing. What turned Barbara off—and what would do the same thing to readers—is the self-consciousness of the writing. By changing spellings so radically, and for no other reason than to show off, I called attention to myself unnecessarily—I intruded between Barbara and the text.

Her reaction might have been annoyance, but for most readers it probably would have been embarrassment ... at the length the writer would go to call attention to himself. The reader becomes embarrassed for the writer, and you know how negative that can be when you want to create a bond with the reader.

Misspellings should be approached the way we handled tricky and jazzy punctuation in Chapter 12: Avoid the urge, if possible, because the results usually don't measure up. The risk of appearing pretentious or obtuse is too severe for what you hope to accomplish. For example:

—If you want a character to answer "yeah," don't write "yeh." Why? Because there isn't much difference in the word sounds, the results are still the same and you've distracted the reader.

—If you start spelling phonetically (*kayble* for "cable," *streem* for "stream"), you'd better have a purpose for it all. It's not enough to want to be "different" because most readers equate being "different" with being odd, and they relegate such techniques to the bone yard of "experimental" writing.

Yet, there are good reasons for deliberately misspelling, and a careful writer can make it work. Mark Twain did it repeatedly with Jim, the runaway slave who formed such a strong bond with Huckleberry Finn. He had Jim mangling syntax as well as mispronouncing words which then, of course, became misspelled: *ðen ... ðat ... noways ... sholy* (for "surely") *... ðey ...* But Jim was un-educated, in the school sense, and it didn't seem odd that he would speak this way or that Mark Twain would write this way. The purpose was to characterize Jim, and it worked.

Sometimes you may misspell in order to develop new words, and again, if you have a purpose, it can work. In my book on censorship I made a modest attempt by combining "book" and "banning" into "bookbanning," which became part of the title. Why did I do it? I thought a single word would depict the dis-agreeable practice more dramatically than allowing it to remain two words. I thought of crimes such as robbery, rape, murder, arson—all single words, and I felt that "bookbanning" was an intellectual crime of the same magnitude and might benefit from this singularity. It would be undiluted and it would be the sim-plest epithet—one word.

Probably, the most extreme misspelling that also served a pur-pose is Anthony Burgess's *A Clockwork Orange*. Here the author developed an entire language that combined obvious misspellings of familiar words with completely new words. In the classic liter-ary sense it was a "tour de force," and because his purpose was to depict a future society and the evolved language they developed, he felt free to misspell or use heretofore-unknown words. For example, Alex, his protagonist, has been arrested and has agreed to therapy to neutralize his violent nature. One of the therapies was to force him to watch scenes of violence over and over. Alex describes what happens:

> And then I found they were strapping my rookers to the chair-arms and my nogas were like stuck to a foot-rest. It seemed a bit bezoomny to me but I let them get on with what they wanted to get on with. If I was to be afree young malchick again ...

Burgess wasn't trying to be "cute," nor was he seeking to be different in order to call attention to himself. He had serious literary purpose, and when that happens, misspellings or recast words meld into the prose and fit easily.

Getting cute with misspellings sometimes spills over into dialogue, too. Writers can forget the basic dialogue rules that take simple conversation and turn it into drama. Dialogue must:

1. move the story along, or
2. develop characterization, or
3. do both of the above.

There are no exceptions; there is no need for any other rule. A writer who forgets these rules will produce uninteresting prose, and when that same writer starts to get cute with dialogue, the uninteresting prose will become a disagreeable burr to the reader in the same way that uncalled for misspellings do.

Phonetically-spelled dialogue is one way it happens (take my *foto*, solve this *puzzel*, let's eat *brokolee*). They confuse more than anything else. Good word choice works better, and if you must deviate from standard spellings (such as using regionalisms or ethnic words or phrases) in order to give the *flavor* of nonstandard speech, do it less rather than more. An occasional usage is fine, a barrage is not. For example, in Kathryn Lynn Davis's historical romance, *Child of Awe*, set around 1500 in Scotland, the author describes a moment of decision for Isabel, one of the characters, who recalls the words of Archibald Campbell and his attitude towards the safety of another character, Muriella:

> ... She'll stay only as long as ye can keep her safe. No' a moment more! Remember, you're sworn ... [then he adds directly to Isabel] and now, so are ye ...

Note the touches of regional dialogue, but note, too, how much more is not regionalized. Only "ye" and "no'" (meaning "not") are made phonetic. And note, too, that the remainder of the passage reads in standard language and word usage. All the author has done is give us the *flavor* of old Scottish, not the full-course meal.

How does a writer know when she starts to become "cute" with dialogue? She calls attention to the dialogue for reasons other than moving the story along or developing characterization. The writer intrudes between the reader and what is on the written page.

> "I—I–I–I c-c-c-an't g-go ..." he stammered.

Does this intrude? We know the speaker stammers, the dialogue tagline tells us that. But it's hard and slow to read. The reader is distracted from the story. What if the writer wrote:

> "I c-can't go," he stammered.

It's not overkill, yet we do get the point. By overemphasizing the stammering in the first example, the writer has called undue attention to himself, and the reader feels jarred.

What if the writer wants to speak to the reader about what the reader has just read?

> "I'm not sure I'm going to make it ..."
> (*Me:* That's today's crisis, ladies and gentlemen)

> "I'm feeling so weak ..."
> (*Me:* The drama builds)

If this type of thing is done carefully, it can work well because the author becomes one of his own characters, and the reader has a live, breathing human to relate to, not simply a created character. But it's so easy to get "cute" with this technique, and then disaster will strike. For example:

"I'm not sure I'm going to make it..."
(*Me*: See how I've tried to add some excitement? This character needs help, but who's going to offer? It's what a wimp would say.)

There's too much author intrusion here, and the effect of the technique is lost. The reader can't help but wonder why the author is explaining so much. The story comes to a complete stop, and the reader's interest will lag. In the hands of an experienced writer, however, the technique can add dimension to the characters and open up the plot, providing the dialogue rules are kept firmly in mind.

But be careful! It's so easy to use grammar and syntax and turn solid dialogue into something "cute" and embarrassing. Whenever you're tempted to be "different" and to play around with spellings and pronunciation or page graphics or author intrusion, take a long, deep breath.

And look yourself in the eye.

Cuteness, after all, can only be a state of mind.

DON'T WAVE AWAY CLICHÉS AND BOTCHED METAPHORS

Up to now we've been on a fairly narrow path with grammar and syntax, rejecting practices that caused awkward writing and tended to push the reader's interest away. Grammar that produced heavy-handed or esoteric results was grammar to be avoided. Syntax that confused word order or created self-conscious prose was obviously a poor choice.

Now, though, we come to one of those aberrations in any writer's list of dos and don'ts because there is nothing absolute in the writer's art, and no matter how certain you might be that a writing technique is cemented into immovability, reality can dislodge it.

Sometimes, frankly, even the most egregious things will work if the circumstances are right. I've described how split infinitives work well, why one-sentence, even one-word paragraphs might be appropriate, and when you should *not* mirror the prose of the most respected writers.

Now it's time to knock away another absolutist writing pillar. *Clichés and botched metaphors are not always wrong or ineffective.* Sometimes they will work and work well, and the careful writer knows when and how to use them.

But first, why you should not use them.

Anyone who has taken a writing class has heard the litany about clichés ... *a lazy way of writing*! "Think creatively!" you're implored. That overused word or phrase can squeeze out freshness

and spontaneity and turn vibrant prose into sentences gasping for breath. You don't want that to happen to what *you* write!

Botched metaphors do the same thing, though they spring from a convoluted sense of imagery instead of a reliance on lazy writing. The effect, however, is usually the same … a reader jarred by inept and inapt writing.

"The kid doesn't cut the mustard," the coach said.

Here is a cliché wrapped in a dead metaphor. We've heard the phrase many times—it offers no fresh insights. An experienced writer would not be caught dead (a cliché, of course) inserting it when the prose is in his authorial voice—that is, when the author is speaking directly to the reader and not through a character. Most of us recognize clichés easily, and it isn't difficult to come up with something more imaginative.

"The kid doesn't need to slow down to stop," the coach said.

Same meaning, same effect, but a different phrase. Gone are the cliché and the botched metaphor—fresh words in their places. The reader might even appreciate the humor.

To "cut the mustard" tries to call up an image, and that is what a metaphor is designed to do. It's a phrase based upon a comparison of two dissimilar items that happen to have the same effect or appearance. In this case, it is the kid's poor level of athletic skill equated with an ability to cut mustard (which is an expression from our Western frontier days meaning to come up to expectations, to be of "the proper mustard"). The comparison must be identical for the metaphor to exist (not simply "like one another" as in the same of a simile), and that is what occurs here. Poor athletic skill and inability to cut mustard are the same, and thus, we have a metaphor.

But it's a "dead" metaphor in the sense that the image is trite, used up, and unclear. Do we picture someone trying to cut mustard? Does it actually *mean* anything?

That's why it's a dead metaphor … it has passed into the language as *idiom*, having been used so much as to carry beyond the

metaphor stage. It has become reborn, and under certain circumstances, it will work well.

Consider this paragraph:

> A story will *flow* if the writer *sculpts* his prose by *melding* syntax and minding the *pulls and tugs* of grammar so that his metaphors will *ring sweetly* and his images become *illuminated* ...

Does a story flow? Does a writer sculpt? Does syntax meld or does grammar have pulls and tugs? Will metaphors ring sweetly and images actually become illuminated? Literally, of course not, but they do work — partially — if you're trying to create some imagery. However, they aren't so creative or unique as to do much by themselves; it's only when they work together in a paragraph that something happens. You could call them "dead" metaphors because they aren't creative enough, standing alone, and they are verbs you've seen or heard many times.

But ... suppose you write the same paragraph as a literal writer might, trying to stay clear of the dead metaphors:

> A story will read better if the writer is careful with his prose, watching his syntax and grammar, and offering good metaphors and clear images ...

This is certainly clear enough, but it sparks no word picture. The earlier version creates images in spite of its problems, and the dead metaphor can come alive again.

There is a place for clichés and botched metaphors, no matter how delicately you may wish to write. The key is to recognize them for what they are and to know when and how to use them. (I'd recommend a word and phrase guide such as *Morris Dictionary of Word and Phrase Origins* by William and Mary Morris. It provides the *real* meanings to idioms, catchphrases and other familiar expressions.) When you're speaking to the reader directly as author, you're presenting yourself in the best possible light, and you should always avoid clichés and botched metaphors because they will put a label on your skill level (mediocre, uninspired, dull, dull, dull!). Examples include the following:

"Rome wasn't built in a day," she said.

"You're waiting for the brass ring," he said.

"I have the patience of Job, you know..."

"Life's no bowl of cherries, it's a jungle out there!"

We've all known people who fall back on clichés when they speak (and when they write!), and it's not uncommon for them to be the butt of a joke. Why not, then, have a character in a story mirror this personality? A cliché-spouting, metaphor-botching character? There's certainly humor in it, but even more than that, there's that reader identification factor. *Most readers do know someone who never found a cliché or botched metaphor he didn't like*!

An experienced writer could develop a character with these traits, and most of us would nod and recall meeting such a person in real life. Here again, even with a botched metaphor, you have reader identification and continued reader interest.

Now add a touch of humor, and you have characterizations that will give any reader pleasure. In the hands of an accomplished writer such as Donald E. Westlake, for instance, clichés and botched metaphors are delightful characterization tools. In his 1983 novel, *Why Me*, he sets a scene in a neighborhood bar in New York City shortly before closing. Several patrons discuss what happens when most people believe something that isn't so:

"What's that? Mass hysteria?"

"No, no" [a patron observes]. "Mass hysteria, that's when everyone's scared of the plague. What you're thinking of is *folie à deux* ..."

"It is?"

[Another observes] "It is not. *Folie à deux* is when you see double."

> A ... regular, asleep till now, lifted his head from the bar to say, "De-
> lirium tremens." Then he lowered his head again ...

Clichés and botched metaphors abound here, but what gives this selection its verve is the humor. The bar patrons can't quite get their meanings to fit, and with each suggestion they move further away. They take a cliché, "mass hysteria," and fix an exotic — though clearly inappropriate — French phrase on it (because folie à deux is a shared delusion by *two* people, only). This becomes a botched metaphor because the two items are not the same, and the comparison doesn't work. If that isn't enough, the French phrase is applied inaccurately, and the effect is to leave us further away from the initial question than when we started. The final touch of humor comes with the response, "delirium tremens," which sums up the nonsense and relegates it to its proper corner. What Westlake does is to use clichés and botched metaphors as character builders, and the more ridiculous he has his characters sound, the funnier they become. The essence is to have characters *argue* about the proper meaning, when all the time we know they haven't the foggiest notion of the proper meaning. He uses clichés and botched metaphors as tools to get his humor across.

And he surely succeeds.

21

DON'T PASSIFY YOUR VERB VOICE

One of my early fiction attempts resulted in a story that I sent to a so-called "men's" magazine. The story was based on an experience I had as an adolescent, but as I fictionalized those real circumstances, I was unaware of neutralizing the natural drama in my story. Somehow, the feeling had come that what I enjoyed as an adolescent I should now feel guilt about as an adult. And because I wrote—as we all do—in alliance with my feelings, my words came sheathed in veils.

When he returned my story, the editor offered these comments:

> You must *understand* the market you are writing for. We want *racehorse* prose, strong phrasing, action, action, action.
>
> Make the reader want to leap off the couch and bull his way into the scene ...

I went over my manuscript in light of what the editor had written and, sure enough, I began to see how I had pulled my prose punches. "He was urged to run his tongue over her finger tip ... He was caressed ... His shirt was slid off ... The pile of clothes was kicked into the corner ..."

It was as if I had removed myself from the direct impact with the action, as if I had softened everything. This is the way I should have phrased things:

> She showed him her finger. "Lick it," she urged ... She caressed him ... She slid his shirt off ... She kicked the pile of clothes into the corner ...

It's action and it moves much more quickly than the first try. I'm not sure if it rises to the "racehorse" level, but it certainly offers a better chance of catching the reader's interest and attention.

And that's the point. I had overlooked a most important grammar effect: verb voice. It does have an impact. For instance:

The ore was pulled to the surface by the hardworking men ...

This is the passive voice because the subject (the ore) gets verbed, it doesn't *do* the verbing. Who does the pulling? The men. Are they the subject? No, they're part of a prepositional phrase at the end.

The men worked to bring the ore to the surface ...

This is the active voice: subject (the men) *does* the verbing (worked). If you compare the two treatments, you'll see that the one with the active verb voice gives more drama and life. In stories such as my early men's magazine try, this was what the editor hoped for, and it's pretty clear why he wanted things this way: *reader identification*. The more action, the more the reader gets into the story.

Note this, however: Racehorse prose isn't the only purpose for using the active voice. It's appropriate any time you want to move things along a bit, any time you want to bring a direct form of writing to the reader. The active voice simplifies things, it makes the subject *act*, and it offers a consistent, direct style.

It also provides a more dramatic form of writing. The active voice creates a word picture more vividly, more spontaneously than does the passive voice. Compare these:

The men skied over the crevasse ... (active voice)

The crevasse was being skied over by the men ... (passive voice)

Obviously, the word picture is more exciting with the active voice. It's shorter, more direct and the event is clear and unambiguous. Fall back on that familiar urging, "show, don't tell!" to discover

why the active voice has so much power. It develops that word picture in the reader's mind. Using an active verb will gain the reader's attention. You can develop an image that will stick in his mind: he *struck* ... she *raced* ... he *yelled* ... she *cried* ...

This is "showing" ... but note: If you have a long narrative passage, and you continue to use active verbs, it might seem you are actually "telling" because of the absence of dramatic effects such as dialogue. Not true though, because in the hands of a savvy writer there can be fine drama with long, narrative (slowly rising tension, for example), and using active verbs is one way to help achieve it. Narrative, however, does run the risk of "telling" if you fall back on passive verbs because the word picture won't be as sharp and the tendency to drift into undramatic prose will arise.

Writers seem to fall into use of the passive voice because it appears to be more comfortable. It's less confrontational certainly. (I once had a student who found he could not develop tension in his stories because he hated confrontations in real life, and each time he tried to work it in a story, he developed a block.) And it doesn't force the writer to be so aggressive. Using the passive voice means being softer, more roundabout, less excitable. No doubt it has appeal, especially for those who wish to develop subtlety in their work.

But it runs the risk of telling rather than showing because it lends itself to greater wordiness and less direct reader anticipation. The passive voice extends the narrative, making it more comfortable to remain in narrative prose. And since it is by nature the less dramatic form, problems with "telling" could arise. Here's a short passage from Rosamond Smith's novel *Soul/Mate* about a killer and his victim on the run:

> They stopped at a trucker's restaurant where Colin, pistol inside his shirt, bought hot food, coffee. They stopped on a lookout point—a "scenic site"—in the Adirondack Mountains not many miles from the Canadian border. Dorothea's mind worked swiftly and with seeming proficiency but to no purpose. She would signal someone ...

Blunder No. 21

All of this is in the active voice, and we get the continuing impression of tension, as well as a clear word picture. But what happens if we rewrite it in the passive voice?

> Hot food, coffee were stopped for and were bought by Colin, pistol inside his shirt, at a trucker's restaurant. A lookout point was stopped at—a "scenic site"—in the Adirondack Mountain not many miles from the Canadian border. Dorothea's mind was being worked swiftly and with seeming proficiency, but to no purpose. Someone would be signaled…

Not only is the passage awkward in the passive voice, but it develops barely an image. We get a much less vivid sense of the tension in the scene *because the personal noun or pronoun is not used as the subject of each sentence*. That's the key. The active voice gets the reader more involved because it tends to personalize things. That creates the image that allows us to "show" instead of "tell."

There is a time for the passive voice, however. It's best illustrated in the context of a sense of pace. If the active voice tends to speed things up, the passive voice tends to slow them down. And the time may come when this is exactly what you want. Perhaps, as with slow motion in films, you wish to strrrreeetch the action to establish characterization, to show position or attitude ("she was touched"…"he was shocked"…) or, as with sound effects onstage, you wish to establish a certain mood or atmosphere. The passive voice, because it elongates the prose, give you time to work these miracles where you can create an effect with simple words:

> The lights were being watched by the man who was being watched by the clerk who was being watched by the owner who was being watched by the police… But who was being watched by the urchin who was being helped to slide behind the fruit stand, and who was being hurt by this simple thievery?

The passive voice has slowed down the watchfulness, and instead of bristling tension (which the active voice would have given us)

there is a rumbling alertness, a lower-case tension. Matters have slowed down—though they are certainly still tense—but the urgency is removed, and the mood has changed. Now you have many more choices about where to take the story; had the active voice been used, you would have been at a high level of tension, and story movement would have been limited. By lowering the voltage, you provide more opportunity.

That's when the passive voice can work.

And it can actually make a stronger statement, if emphasis is placed on the object, instead of the do-er. For example:

His fortune was made in the stock market.

He made his fortune in the stock market.

The first selection, which emphasizes the "fortune" (the object) is stronger, even though the verb is in passive voice. The second selection, which uses the active voice, emphasizes the "doer" as the subject and relegates "fortune" to a less primary goal.

It's easy to remember the difference: *The writer works the active voice … The passive voice was worked by the writer.*

Active is better, but not always.

Don't Hide Parallelisms in the Prose

William Zinsser said that every good writer should be part poet, "always listening to what he writes." You know by now that word sounds affect the reader even when she scans the pages of a book. The reader hears as well as reads, and this gives the written word a double charge.

The poet seeks to stamp our senses with ringing self-awareness, and the available tool is words, nothing but words. Choice of words is crucial, certainly, but so is their juxtaposition.

> *Crack!* The hull snapped ... *Whoosh*! The water flooded in ...
> Oh! the doomed men cried ...

A straightforward action description, using active verbs and physical exclamation. The word picture forms clearly. Now see what happens when I change things around:

> The hull snapped with a crack, and whoosh! came the water while the doomed men could but utter a collective oh!...

The sense of immediacy is lost; the sense of drama and tension is reduced. And it's because of how the words are placed in the sentence. In the second example, "crack" is the object in a prepositional phrase; "whoosh" is an adverb; "oh!" is the object of a verb. Each sound of exclamation is used in a different grammatical construction, and because they all convey exclamations, their varied use is unsettling.

There is no unity in the phrasing. Unless there was deliberate intention to do it this way to achieve some special purpose, the lack of unity marks a writer who isn't paying attention to the word sounds.

It comes down to style again. What we're talking about is rhythm and cadence, the *beat* and the *sound*. Prose should flow, and its smoothness is directly related to how it plays on the ear; a style that expresses itself in herky-jerky fashion, a rhythm that jars the reader, will irritate. And few writers want to do that.

What you have to understand are so-called "unities" when it comes to certain phrasing. That is, you need to think in "parallelisms" because this is the surest way to avoid botching your rhythm and style. Above all else, you want to keep your prose smooth and flowing.

"Parallelisms" are words and phrases in series that either answer one another or coincide with one another. Back to my eighth-grade teacher a moment … On the blackboard she writes a lengthy sentence from a novel we are reading, and she places brackets around the first clause, then brackets around the second clause, then brackets around the third clause …

"Are these clauses the same?" she asks.

"They do the same thing," someone volunteers.

"Different words," another offers.

The teacher waves us to silence. "They aren't identical," she says, "but they are parallel." She rewrites them on the board, one under the other. "Same rhythm," she says, sounding each one out in turn, "same parts of speech, same general length. And"—she points back to the sentence itself— "they aren't spread all over the page …"

Parallelisms seem easy enough because they appeal to a natural order, and all of us have some internal striving for that. Writing without order is chaos, as is a disordered life, and if you write something you wish others to read, you must produce words and phrases that hang together. Parallelisms have a way

of helping to do that by creating a rhythm and cadence which the reader can assume. The parallelisms work together, side by side, to establish that rhythm.

Let's go back to poetry for a moment. It's here that parallelism is clearest. In Rudyard Kipling's poem, "The Young British Soldier," he attempts to explain what barracks life is, and after each stanza, he finishes with a five- or six-word phrase, such as: "Fit, fit, fit for a soldier ... " "Bad, bad, bad for the soldier ..." "Fool, fool, fool of a soldier ..." "Beer, beer, beer for the soldier ..." "Curse, curse, curse of a soldier ..." "Wait, wait, wait like a soldier ..."

These are parallelism, and what Kipling was striving for was a repetitious sound and rhythm to give an idea of marching and cadence. It is, after all, a poem about soldiers, so why not add to the mood by developing parallel phrasing?

In prose, the problem is that many of us don't see parallelisms when they stare us in the face. You probably don't even look for them, and the result is that your writing can slip out of rhythm and you're not aware of it. The simplest type of parallelism is the series; most of us have used this again and again: "He spoke to me harshly, and I answered in kind and then I left the room ..."

This is simple straightforward narrative with each clause approximately the length of the others and denoting action. Although the opening clause isn't preceded by a conjunction, there is balance here (you could almost infer an opening conjunction, couldn't you?) and an easy rhythm. You write compound sentences all the time, and as you add clauses, it's important to make them parallel, especially when they are in a series, because it establishes rhythm. See how this reads if you ignore the parallelism:

> "He spoke to me harshly; however, my anger made me answer in kind, while the room was no place I wanted to be ..."

It's bumpy prose, the cadence is broken, and the writer is singled out for the dos and don'ts list in a creative writing class.

A common parallelism is a series of phrases, each following a preposition, and it's obvious why this should be treated carefully. The rhythm is fragile. Remember how Abraham Lincoln concluded his Gettysburg Address:

> ... that this nation, under God, shall have a new birth of freedom, and that government *of* the people, *by* the people, *for* the people, shall not perish from the earth. (emphasis added)

Note that he didn't use the same preposition to introduce each phrase, only that he used a one-syllable preposition. Note, too, that the parallelisms are buried within the sentence. They don't comprise the entire sentence—there are other phrases there, as well. But the parallelisms are about the same length, and the rhythm reaches out for the reader (and the audience!). Suppose, however, Abraham Lincoln paid little heed to parallelisms. Then, he might have ended this way:

> ... that this nation for the people, under God, with a government of the people, shall have a new birth of freedom by the people and shall not perish from the earth.

Fine sentiments, to be sure, but they have no ring of cadence, no particular rhythm, no poetic touch. It took conscious development of a parallelism to bring out the impact, and the latter version nullifies it. A major reason why is that the parallel clauses are not close to one another on the page. They are separated, and their impact is certainly affected because the cadence is broken. Parallelisms, especially those in a series, must follow one another, or be so close that their rhythm and the cadence can't fade away. Separate them by another clause, and they lose their significance.

Parallelisms come in other forms, one of which is where the clauses or phrases *answer* one another. They aren't in a series, they don't coincide with one another, but they create a rhythm because they dovetail. A situation in contrast would be one way of doing

this: violent storm outside, quiet tension inside ... a singular pro-
posal, a plural response ("Why must I suffer?" ... "Your victims
have an answer!"). See how Walt Whitman handles responding
portions in his *Specimen Days & Collect*, a battlefield recollection
of Chancellorsville during the Civil War:

> The night was very pleasant, at times the moon shining out full and clear,
> all Nature so calm in itself, the early summer grass so rich, and foliage
> of the trees—yet there was the battle raging, and many good fellows
> lying helpless ... and every minute amid the rattle of muskets and crash
> of cannon ... the red life-blood oozing out from heads or trunks or limbs
> upon that green and dew-cool grass ...

It's nature and man, peace and war, beauty and horror ... a peace-
ful, pleasant evening, then depicted through the suffering of
fighting men. Note the dovetail parallelism: The gentle portrait
is offered first, then the violence responds to it; the grass was "so
rich," and later there was red blood oozing "upon that green and
dew-cool grass"; the two sections are not identical in length, but
they are portrayed with active verbs, and the final clauses in each
section offer poetic image. Each section fills the other, and this is
the point of parallelisms that *answer* one another: They broaden
the scene, and they do it better when they keep the rhythm.

Awareness can bring parallelism to life, and this can produce
a cadence which can develop a rhythm which can create an image
which can excite a reader.

23

Don't Ignore Effective Italics

One of the things we learned as teenagers was that emotions could be expressed in outsized fashion. Recall the wide mood swings and the surging impetuosity that often careened into self-inflicted crisis. Remember your verbal characterizations (which often ended with hyperbole):

"*Honestly*, it was *too* awful!"

"He's a *complete* jerk!"

"A *monster* party, a *fantastic* band!"

Vocally underlining a word or phrase comes naturally (and frequently) with teenagers, but their concerns might not be those of the serious writer seeking publication. The serious writer knows there are many ways to establish prose emphasis, among them active verbs, strong adjectives, capitalization, and exclamation points. The serious writer also knows that overindulging in any of them will create a fog of indifference with the reader. Emphasis used regularly becomes no emphasis at all, and with the slackening pace, readers will slowly turn away.

In written prose, italics are often used to supply emphasis, and they provide a change of pace in the way words *look* on the page. But italics can do more than offer emphasis. They can create a new voice within the prose, a different voice. In my book, *Bookbanning in America*, which deals with censorship, I explored how simple words of prose can become The Word with symbol and action intertwined. Note how I use italics:

> A bookbanner facing this adversary could have only one reaction—*ban the book!* ... Four-letter words, for example. *Such language is fit for the sewer. Children shouldn't be exposed to that sort of thing* ...

By italics I inserted the bookbanner into the writing, and I've characterized him through dialogue. The italics represent what the bookbanner might be saying or thinking, and they create drama and change of pace. Italics also add interest for the reader.

But be careful. As with italics used for emphasis, italics presenting a new voice should not be overused. The same risk is there: The new voice loses its special appeal if it appears too frequently. I know because I thought I could do it with *Bookbanning in America*. I wanted to end each of the first ten chapters with an italicized update and a change of voice. The selections would have run three to four pages.

My editor shook her head after reading the submitted manuscript. "It's too much," she said. "Reading italics is harder than reading Roman script; the reader will grow impatient. Keep it short."

"I want to shift voices," I said.

"We'll leave a space between the two portions. It'll be obvious to the reader, and you won't need italics."

She was right.

Yet italics are a valuable tool, and they can influence style in dramatic ways. One of the most creative users of italics is Tom Wolfe, the journalist and novelist who some credit with developing the "new journalism" in the 1960s that changed the face of nonfiction. What Wolfe did was to use italics as a dramatic tool and to expand the universe of characterization and story line. A piece of nonfiction was no longer a straight recitation of things actually happening—the facts, the solid facts. Wolfe wanted to get inside the heads of the people he was writing about, and he felt that if

he came to know them well enough, he could do just that. In *The Right Stuff*, his book about the space program, he described a flight to reach Mach 1 by test pilot Chuck Yeager in the late 1940s:

> "Had a mild buffet there ... jes the usual instability ..."
> *Jes the usual instability?*
> Then the X-1 reached the speed of .96 Mach, and that incredible caint-hardlyin' aw-shuckin' drawl said:
> "Say, Ridley ... make a note here, will ya?" *(if you ain't got nothin' better to do)* " ... elevator effectiveness *regained*."

Wolfe is in Chuck Yeager's head and his italics show us that. He has expanded our level of awareness: Not only do you get Yeager's direct reactions to what he's experiencing, but you also get Tom Wolfe's reactions to Yeager's experience ... you understand how the writer feels about what Yeager says and does. The italics shift the focus from character to writer and then back again, and the effect is to broaden your understanding and your identification. Wolfe's sympathies are obvious, especially with the second italics passage, and there's nothing wrong with that. In fact, the more sympathetic the portrayal, the more developed the character will be, and you know that reader identification will follow.

Note, too, how Wolfe's italics passages stay consistent with Yeager's dialogue style — laconic, unruffled, colloquial — even though it's Tom Wolfe and not Chuck Yeager who is speaking. Here again, this enhances character portrayal and provides a more developed prose style. You come to see Yeager, not only through his own words but through his thought processes and projections *as Tom Wolfe imagines them to be.*

Obviously, overuse of italics creates the same problems as the long, uninterrupted narrative — it's a matter of overkill. Think of italics as butterflies that might swoop across the page, allow them to flit about, land here and there, softly, gently; don't treat them as a blanket that must spread itself across the entire page. The butterfly approach will bring a dash of color; the blanket approach will darken everything.

Sometimes, an inventive writer will go beyond Tom Wolfe's subtle intrusion, making no attempt to portray the character in another voice, making no attempt to limit the dialogue. In this case, italics are the author who then becomes a complete character in the story.

Take a look at this passage from Joan Didion's *Democracy*, a story of the Vietnam War and its aftermath on a politically well-connected American family. Didion, from time to time, puts herself right into the story, not attempting to disguise her participation. In the second chapter, she writes:

> Call me the Author.
> *Let the reader be introduced to Joan Didion, upon whose character and doings much will depend of whatever interest these pages may have, as she sits at her writing table in her own room in her own house on Welbeck Street.*
> So Trollope might begin this novel ...

When Didion shifts focus or point of view to herself, see how she uses italics, how she even mentions herself by name. There's no subtlety here (insofar as the author becomes a character in the story), and Didion doesn't try to disguise herself in the vernacular and the appearance of another character. She is part of the story, as author of course, but also as a character, and by doing this she's able to add substance because she gives the reader still another point of view to ponder. Not only do you see the story through the eyes of other characters, but you also see the story through the eyes of its author, whose point of view might be—and often is—different. This is how you give body to any story and keep the reader interested.

24

DON'T REPEAT
WITHOUT RELEVANCE

Tautology!

Redundancy!

Most of us have endured these grammatical criticisms, especially when trying to pass an English composition course. Sometimes they seemed to be the English teacher's second favorite remark (after "This is not a complete sentence!"), and the comments sounded so severe. Tautology! It was a term of art, not an unflappable expression such as "overwritten" or "cause and effect don't agree" or "comma needed."

Redundancy! It propelled a rolling threat, aimed at the heart of what you wrote. This was no casual criticism because it touched your style, and you know that it meant it was important.

When you're redundant or tautological, it means you've written the same thing using different words—in close proximity. It means you're repeating yourself when there's no reason for it.

It also means your personal editing skills could stand renewal, because repeating yourself on the written page is one of those events you should guard against—always! It's the sort of thing that a reader will pick up and ponder over …*didn't this writer say it before?* And, convinced it's true, the reader will see the writer as disorganized and uninteresting.

When I speak of good, clean prose, of grammatically correct phrasing, I'm talking about writing that has no redundancies (among other things) and no awkward, self-conscious parts.

You're carried forward by the lilt of the writer's style where words and phrases have purpose, and where the music of words will create a harmony of word sounds. In simple writer-editor language, writing such as this "works."

But remember it's *style* you're really considering, and you don't want to get bogged down in a maze of rules and procedures. Your individuality makes itself known through your style, and sometimes the techniques that don't work for one writer might work for another. Here's the opening to Edgar Allan Poe's "The Fall of the House of Usher":

> During the whole of a dull, dark, and soundless day in the autumn of the year, when the clouds hung oppressively low in the heavens, I had been passing alone, on horseback, through a singularly dreary tract of country, and at length found myself, as the shades of evening drew on, within view of the melancholy House of Usher....

Could Ernest Hemingway or Philip Roth write these lines? Style is the key, and the way Poe wrote is not the way another would write.

So we start with a given: tautologies and redundancies are bad. BUT let's not carry it too far because repetitive words and phrasing, or even repetitive punctuation, can have a worthy place. It all depends on how they are to be used. There's a difference between a redundancy and a repetitive phrase — one repeats using different words and different sounds but says the same thing; the other repeats with identical words and sounds. One adds little to style, the other may provide a stylistic lift.

The alert writer, of course, knows the difference and how to squeeze out the best results.

> "I'm not here to hurt you," he said.
> *Sure.*
> "I don't even want to be here."
> *Sure.*

"I could throw this gun away ..."

Sure, sure, sure, sure ...

The tension in this exchange is palpable, and it's shoved along by the repeated use of "sure." The technique accomplishes at least two things: it provides a second voice (the speaker and the commentator), which creates drama through tension, and it allows comment on the credibility of the speaker. Using a simple repetitive word keeps things narrow and tightly focused—and more easily managed.

Note, too, how the effect of "sure" builds each time it's used. After the first dialogue passage it amounts, perhaps, to a raised eyebrow ... but by the second "sure" it becomes a more insistent challenge ... and after the third dialogue passage, it represents strong disagreement.

It doesn't have to be a single word, of course; it could be a phrase. Remember Kurt Vonnegut's "and so it goes ..." that we discussed in Chapter 3? He used the phrase at the end of chapters or scenes to underscore the banality of horrific events, and with each use the imagery was enhanced. If he had used it only once, it wouldn't have had the impact that repeating it produced. And each time the phrase appeared, the reader pondered its effect ... and the image grew more vivid. It's similar to painting a landscape: With each color, with each stroke, the portrait takes shape until it becomes an entire, completed scene, and we understand what the painter is seeking to tell us. With each "and so it goes ..." Vonnegut did the same thing, yet his message remained incomplete until the final repetitive phrase appeared. Then we fully understood.

Repeating words or phrases is a useful technique because it can enhance both meaning and impact without lengthy dialogue or discourse. The repetitive word or phrase itself provides the message the writer wishes to develop.

But that doesn't mean *any* word or *any* phrase should be repeated. There must be a purpose, a reason why the word or phrase is re-

peated, a connection to the major thrust of the storyline. Repetition without relevance offers little and will only confuse the reader.

I know this well because I was guilty of it in a nonfiction book manuscript. In one chapter, there was a profile of a man who had acquired substantial power in his profession. He was politically astute and manipulative while offering a hearty, disarming presence, and he seemed unconcerned whether means and ends were compatible. In his cynicism there was corruptibility, and I wanted to get that across.

But how? Saying it outright had the disadvantage of making it undramatic. Any book—fiction or nonfiction—that pulls dramatic punches is asking for trouble. I wanted to portray this *dramatically*!

Perhaps a repetitive phrase would do. There was nothing he, himself, said that I could use, nothing he repeated over and over. But I could inject myself, as writer, into the story and offer a second voice. I knew that he had achieved power within his organization through political manipulation.

Politics corrupts, I decided.

And as I wrote the chapter, I injected the phrase *politics corrupts!* when it seemed appropriate, usually after self-congratulatory dialogue or a description of his various successes.

Politics corrupts!

I was pleased, and I remained so even after a second rewrite. I sent a draft of the chapter to my editor (perhaps my subconscious was trying to tell me something—unless specifically asked, I never sent in drafts), and her response was clear and to the point—the repetitive phrase tended to confuse things. Remove it.

I put the manuscript away for a few days and then reread it. As I faced that ogre of author's pride (which we all have and which only the surest among us can control), I began to see what the editor meant. The repetitive phrase did not extend the meaning of what was already in the manuscript because the character, himself, through his own words or actions, had already made clear that politics corrupts. Adding my (author's) voice was superfluous and actually tended to irritate the reader because it was telling the reader something the reader already knew. There was nothing in *politics corrupts!* either by meaning or by impact, that was new.

It grieved me because I had been so pleased with myself. I saw this as a sophisticated way to bring out the full range of disagreeable characteristics, something different, something unusual.

But it didn't work, and I learned a valuable lesson.

Repeating a word or phrase can add luster to your work, but it must be approached gingerly. Its most obvious purpose is to add emphasis (as in *yes, yes, yes, yes!!!*), but be careful: it's so easy to cross the line to overemphasis, and that means you have fallen into the trap of melodrama. The key is to see whether enough emphasis exists already, and whether you are repeating only to be gratuitous. When in doubt, avoid the repetitive word or phrase because the dramatic effect is probably built in already. Emphasize to make a point, and weigh the dramatic effect of what you emphasize. If it's melodramatic, it's better to leave it out.

Obviously, the words or phrases you repeat don't have to be in juxtaposition; they can come pages, even chapters, apart, but they must set up some continuity and purpose. Unlike redundancies and tautologies, they must add to the prose, give the work something it wouldn't otherwise have had. To accomplish this, you must be both a sensitive writer and critical editor. You must create or choose the repetitive word or phrase, and weigh its usefulness and purpose. If you find satisfaction both ways, then the repetition "works."

25

DON'T ASSUME AUTHOR ABSOLUTISM

"Write what you know!" Experienced writers have been preaching that for as long as the creative urge has spurred the creative judgment. What's most familiar is what you understand best, and what you'll write about best.

But consider this: What you produce *can* be improved upon, in spite of the fact that no one else could possibly know as much about the subject: *my* story, *my* experience, *my* creation.

Someone else might be able to make it better.

Denying this leads only to author absolutism: *I know better what I want to say and how to say it.*

I recall a conversation with the editor of a major regional magazine. I had suggested a profile of a controversial political figure based upon some unpublished information and my ability to interpret it. All the editor knew about me was what was on my list of writing credits and the one-page outline I had provided. We had not met before.

"You understand this stuff?" he asked, referring to the date I showed him.

"I've studied it carefully," I said.

"But can you *write* it well?"

I was surprised. I assumed that since I knew my subject, I would produce good prose.

"I know what I'm writing about," I said.

He put a hand on my shoulder. "Experts I don't want or need," he said. "I'd rather get ten thousand words on how to tie a shoe-

lace from Norman Mailer than have an expert describe the same thing in half the space."

It's a comment I've never forgotten. Experts on anything, including on yourself and on what you know, are only one side of the writing equation. Equally important, if not more so, is whether you can write well what you know. And that leads back to author absolutism, because we do tend to confuse a proprietary sense over our own words and phrases with what we know.

It simply doesn't follow that because you know your subject better than anyone else, you'll be able to write about it better than anyone else. What you know are *facts*; what you have to turn them into is *drama*. You have to make things interesting for the reader, and you can't assume you have all the answers.

"I like that word," you insist in your author absolutism, or "That paragraph says exactly what I want to get across." But the truth is, in matters of grammar (language use and abuse, punctuation, style and syntax), the writer is not always correct. Others sometimes know better.

The difficult thing is to make yourself believe it. If you think a series of ellipses should be scattered through a manuscript, not merely to demonstrate the passing of time but to add suspense or heightened awareness, you might have a hard time with an editor who found the technique distracting. Yet a confident writer would not throw up his hands and walk away without considering the alternatives. At the least, a suggestion for a change in grammar technique should force you to rethink your original selection.

Most of us have a particular sensitivity when it comes to that elusive notion, "style," because it is the one thing that can bring us notoriety. Writers are known for their "styles" ... Jay McInerny, for instance, or Elmore Leonard or Toni Morrison or Nadine Gordimer. They are recognizable by the way they string words together, and no one else does it quite the same way.

In striving to develop your style, you may sometimes get pinned by the author-absolutism urge because you feel proprietary about your own words and phrases ... "changing that paragraph will ruin the effect I want!" ... "you don't understand the way I want things to flow" ... Style is what sets you apart, and you're acutely conscious whenever there's a challenge.

Even to the picayune point of where to put commas and periods. If it might influence "style," you might rise in righteous anger and demand that it be left alone. You may see your personal "style" under attack, and console yourself that you should fight back because, after all, who else knows as much about what you're trying to do? Who else *understands*?

Style has a grammar face, and that's what some writers don't understand. Style is made up of a lot of little things, such as parallel clauses and vibrant colloquialism. It's not a broad cloak of beautiful words or exciting phrases thrown on a page. It is the *way* the words are strung together that gives each of us a "style."

But there's no style that is absolute and untouchable. Every style can be improved.

A friend once asked me to look at a novel he had been working on for over a year. It was a suspense story, he told me, entwined with a love affair that would influence the plot. The main characters, a man and a woman, were from completely different backgrounds, and my friend assumed that this alone would add tension to the story.

"What I need is some grammar help," he said. "I think the story moves well and the plot builds nicely. But I want my syntax to shine, too."

He sounded like he wanted copyediting help, which didn't thrill me. "Let me have a look," I said.

Within twenty pages I knew there were problems — and they weren't copyediting problems. The suspense simply wasn't there. Whatever tension he tried to develop was dissipated by

poetic character portrayals and lengthy descriptive narrative. In suspense literature if the reader hasn't been grabbed in the first few pages (some writers say by the first page or even the first paragraph), the reader has been lost. That's what happened here, though I continued reading.

Unfortunately, there was little change. Ill-fitted for a suspense novel, the languid style was more in keeping with a narrative poem. The characters moved and spoke in desultory fashion; events developed almost as after-thoughts; the love affair that was supposed to spring the story forward seemed like a slow-motion mating dance.

The truth was ... nothing much happened. As a suspense novel, it wouldn't work. Period.

"I think you need a rewrite," I said as kindly as I could.

"I never was much good with grammar," he answered.

"It's your style," I said. "It needs rethinking." I told him he should provide more action and cut back on passive verbs and lengthy description. "Have the characters confront one another, have the characters confront their situation ..."

"I wanted help with syntax," he murmured.

"Style and syntax go together," I said.

"Grammar help, that's all."

"That's what I'm trying—"

"No, you're not," he bristled. "No one's going to rewrite my story."

"Grammar ..." I began.

"Forget it," he answered, gathering up the manuscript. "No one's going to rewrite my book."

No one published it either.

DON'T WRAP CHARACTERS IN THE SAME GRAMMAR BLANKET

Much has been written about how to spark life into characters, but all the advice, all the tips, all the so-called answers come down to one thing ... for a character to have life he must be *memorable*. There must be something about that character that will stick in the reader's mind, that will set that character apart from any other character. It doesn't matter what the memorable characteristic is (it could be a physical mannerism, for example, or a particular like or dislike), but the point is that there must be *something* the reader can fasten upon.

And this memorable something should not be duplicated in the other characters. It must be unique to one character. Think of Joseph Heller's *Catch-22* and the roster of weird characters that included Milo Minderbinder, the entrepreneurial captain who figured the war was a time to make money, not kill people. Heller characterized him so broadly as to turn him into a caricature, but no one will ever forget Milo Minderbinder. He was the quintessential war profiteer, even if he was wearing the uniform of the United States Army.

What made Milo memorable was that Heller did not draw another character this way—Milo was the only war profiteer on the scene. He could fill any request, no matter how absurd—for chocolate-covered cotton, for instance—for a price. Readers don't forget a character like this.

The way a character speaks, how she reacts, is one good way to make a character memorable. But it doesn't work if other char-

acters also speak and react the same way. There's nothing unique for a reader to visualize.

"He's uglier than an outhouse rat ..."

"He's dumber than a box of rocks ..."

"He's heavier than a dead minister ..."

If one character were prone to expressions such as these, the reader would chuckle because she'd come to know him. She could picture such a character, perhaps even "hear his voice." She'd understand both the attributes and the limitations in such a person.

But if there were more than one character using expressions like these, where would that leave the reader? Confused probably, and certainly not as sympathetic because the characters had lost their uniqueness. They were without individuality.

The way a character uses grammar reflects his individuality. As a writer, you have to understand how important it is to keep the individuality of your characters, and one way to accomplish this is by the way they speak and the grammar they use. Dialogue can be a remarkable tool for developing characterization, if you're careful about how you use it.

No better example can be found than in the exchanges between Huckleberry Finn and the runaway slave, Jim, in Mark Twain's classic, *The Adventures of Huckleberry Finn*. Jim, with no formal education, speaks a patois that mixes syntax, word-meanings and word sounds; his grammar, to our refined ears, is atrocious:

"Well, den, dey ain't no sense in a cat talkin' like a man. Is a cow a man? —er is a cow a cat?"

"Well, den, she ain't got no business to talk like either er the yuther of 'em ..."

Huck, while hardly a model English speaker, certainly keeps his grammar more in check, and a good thing, too! Imagine the chaos

on the page if both Huck and Jim spoke in the same manner—if they both fractured the rules of grammar.

In the first place, you'd have a hard time figuring out who was speaking; then, both characters would lose their uniqueness and their special allure. You'd simply find them less compelling to read about and enjoy. And perhaps most important, it's a rare reader who will be content to wade through convoluted grammar in dialogue passage after dialogue passage. One character using fractured grammar presents a challenge and a spark ... but two or three characters speaking the same way turns the trickle into a torrent, and the reader loses interest.

Jim, though, is the only character fracturing grammar so completely, and because of this, he occupies a special place in the book and in the minds of readers. You see him, through his speech patterns, uneducated yet somehow dignified, inarticulate yet somehow wise, and you sense him growing in your mind. But if another character spoke the way he did, much of his charm would vanish.

It's no different than overusing italics (which we touched on in Chapter 23). What is attractive in small doses becomes less so the more it is presented. We called it *overkill* with italics, and the same label can be applied here: Easy does it with fractured grammar, but it has its place and it shouldn't be overlooked.

The point is that people—and characters in a story—think differently, talk differently, use different words, shade their meanings differently. I have a friend who wishes (obsessively) that he were an Englishman. The fact he was born and raised in West Virginia does not prevent him from larding his conversations with "tram" ... "I'll ring you up" ... "telly" ... "sshhedule" (for schedule). Of course it's ludicrous at times, and I've told him so, but he's unfazed. "I am what I am," he says with undeniable logic.

But if he and I were two characters in a story, our speech patterns would reflect our different approaches to language. His

grammar and mine are not the same (neither is our approach to syntax), and on the pages of a book that's fine.

"Who're you picking for the pennant this year?" I might ask.

"Not a fig's interest," he might respond. "The football pools, dear boy, *that's* reality."

"Baseball's the American pastime," I might point out.

"Based on British rounders." He slips on his coat. "Ta-ta..."

The fact that our vocabularies are different gives each of us an individuality a writer could build upon. The more distinct our speech patterns, our grammar, even our colloquialisms, the more real we become to the reader. The way we speak opens the door to other reactions we could have. For example, a character who thinks in—and lards his dialogue with—sports metaphors would naturally see a developing situation this way:

From the entrance to the big lot he surveyed the maze of parked cars. Left field, he remembered, deep left field, that's where he'd parked. The pitch to send him on this wild-goose chase had been a curve he'd seen coming a long way off. They want to stop him, they better throw some high, hard ones...

If no other character in the story thinks or speaks in this manner, we have created someone memorable (at least in the writing technique sense), and the reader should be grateful. Word choice alone can do it.

Take a look at John Irving's *A Prayer for Owen Meany*, which uses a classic grammar technique to distinguish between characters. Owen is tiny in size but with a prodigious voice, and to give that voice special prominence and the character memorable effect, Irving capitalizes every line of Owen Meany's dialogue. For example, here are Owen and the rector's wife rehearsing the annual Christmas pageant. Owen speaks:

"YOU COWS, JUST REMEMBER, YOU'RE SUPPOSED TO BE 'LOWING,' NOT MILLING AROUND."

"I don't want the cows 'lowing' *or* milling around," Barb Wiggin said ...

"LAST YEAR YOU HAD TURTLEDOVES *COOING*," Owen reminded her ...

The emphatic effect of the capitalization brings the character of Owen to life and provides a flesh and blood image. That's not to say that Owen wouldn't be memorable even without the capitalization; John Irving is too good a writer not to distinguish between his characters by what they say as well as by the way they say it. But the capitalization adds something special. It offers a particular insight no other writing technique could offer. In the process, the character of Owen Meany comes through clearer than it might have otherwise. You picture tiny Owen Meany WITH THE BIG, BIG VOICE!

27

DON'T NEGLECT GRAMMAR WHEN MOOD AND ATMOSPHERE CHANGE

By now you should be at ease with the notion that grammar can influence style and style can influence grammar. What you write and how you write are interdependent. But the uses of grammar go beyond its effect on style. Grammar is a "tool" in that it can remake or redesign a prose passage. Grammar can "fix" a piece of writing just as surely as a hammer or saw can turn a rough board into a tabletop or chair leg.

> She carried fruit in a basket on top of her head apples bananas peaches melon her arms lightly extended for balance and grace and between her fingers she twirled multicolored cloth reds blues oranges greens ...

What's needed here, obviously, is commas, and when you insert them, the undisciplined rush of words develops order and meaning. The comas don't imprint the style, except to make it readable, but they do "fix" the passage and make it understandable.

And grammar deals with language use and abuse, too—italics, for example, or over-reliance on the thesaurus—and its impact can be impressive. Think of grammar in the broad sense, as a way for developing good writing and not as a method for limiting or controlling expression. Grammar should be both flexible and innovative, and the savvy writer understands that.

The broad approach to grammar works particularly well when you're trying to develop mood and atmosphere. A writer who isn't conscious of mood or atmosphere runs the risk of creating a scene

that doesn't blend well, and the result will please no one. Mood and atmosphere—the emotional pitch of the scene—is what action plays against, and, handled well, the story will have substance and drama and impact.

For example, an appeal to the senses is one good way to develop a mood or create an atmosphere:

> An acrid odor seemed to rise from the box, stinging his nostrils with memory... grandmother and her homemade laundry soap, clothes that smelled sour but looked clean...

The mood created here is one of nostalgia, and it's developed by recalling smells from earlier times. I could as easily have used an appeal to taste or sight or hearing to set up the nostalgia, but the key is to see that by creating the nostalgia I have changed the mood and atmosphere in the story. The change has been helped along by introducing an appeal to our sense of smell.

Many times little more is needed. The senses can portray a new mood or atmosphere quite well. Grammar technique influences how well mood or atmosphere can be depicted, and when mood or atmosphere changes, *grammar technique should change, too*!

Because it will have the effect of intensifying the change in mood or atmosphere. There's no reason to shift to neutral with grammar technique or to avoid adding to the impact of the changes. Grammar is a tool, remember, and like any tool it can be used in different ways under different circumstances. Suppose, for example, you've been developing a lengthy descriptive passage where the text moves along in an unhurried fashion, and you want the reader to feel a congenial mood.

You might use:

—compound sentences
—passive verbs
—multi-sentenced paragraphs
—familiar words and phrases

All of these will help to develop a "friendly" writing style because they don't jar the reader or cause abrupt changes in the prose. The reader feels comfortable, and this is the mood the writer wants to develop.

Take compound sentences. They tend to create a narrative effect because they tack two or three or more compatible thoughts together by means of conjunctions, and the effect on the reader is like that of a flowing brook — harmonious comfort. This makes the grammar "friendly."

Or take familiar words and phrases. It's certainly easier to read the prose of John Updike than it is to fathom the style and meaning of Anthony Burgess because Updike tends to write in a conventional idiom, and we're more at ease while reading him. That doesn't mean, of course, that Updike won't serve us uncongenial writing (*The Witches of Eastwick* is but one example), only that his general style is not to jar us. He doesn't "create" new words or stretch for esoteric phrasing that might cause us to scratch our heads. The magic Updike weaves is in the subtlety of his descriptions and the soft realism of his dialogue. He gets our attention with a light touch, not a heavy blow.

Anthony Burgess is different. In *A Clockwork Orange,* he developed a new glossary of word meanings, and his characters spoke in unfamiliar idiom. But note what Burgess accomplished (see Chapter 19 for an example of how he wrote). His subject was disturbing and so was his style. His grammar technique consisted of using unfamiliar words and phrasing (among other things); this had its effect on style ... and on the book's mood and atmosphere. It injected a sinister undercurrent. He melded grammar and style well to achieve this effect.

Suppose you wish to create a loving, romantic scene. It's obvious you wouldn't want to jar the reader or develop turmoil that would impede intimacy. Punctuation, for example ... exclamation points, italics, capitalization, dashes. These tend to emphasize words and phrases so they stand out from the text, and when that happens, intimacy dissolves:

> Her hair had a soft, honey smoothness, a blend with her rich tan. LIPS THAT SLOPED WITH PASSION, eyes of lilac blossom—such things always stood out for him. He knew they would touch, and it was what he wanted!

There's no need for the emphasis because the scene develops sufficient romantic appeal through the use of sensuous words and phrases such as "soft, honey" and "lilac blossom," as well as compound or longer sentences. The effort is to develop congenial writing, and it works better if you avoid punctuation that interrupts the prose instead of merging with it. Try reading the above paragraph without the capitalization, dash, and exclamation point.

Moves smoother, doesn't it?

Grammar technique can also create other moods. Perhaps you want abruptness instead of gentleness. Grammar can add to tension or conflict in the same way it can develop a congenial mood. For example, in Chapter 21 we looked at the effects of active and passive verbs, and we saw that active verbs tended to move the story along while passive verbs tended to slow things down. Where you wish to develop tension, you would lean to active verbs, and excitement should flourish:

> He *came*, he *saw*, he *conquered*!

Suppose you want to do the same thing with sentence length. The shorter the sentence the more tension you tend to create and the quicker the pace becomes:

> He walked down the stairs. Clip-clop, his steps sounded. The air stank. The darkness blanketed him. His neck hairs tingled. His mouth tasted metallic…

Try to make this into one or two longer sentences and see things slow down. The abruptness of the quick sentences builds the tension, the *streeeettcchhing* of the phrases reduces it.

It works the same way with incomplete sentences. Their fragmentary nature makes them abrupt in the same way that a sudden noise or exclamation does:

Two voices only. Old/young.

Why him? A loser's prize.

Sorry, pal. His turn tonight.

This character's interior monologue is in sentence fragments because most of us think this way—not in complete sentences. If you add verbs and prepositional phrases, it would slow things down and the abrupt mood would dissipate. Using sentence fragments will pick up the pace (it doesn't have to be limited to interior monologue) and add a staccato rhythm.

And there are grammar tools that can add a mood of tension. Take a look at paragraphing. When you're in a narrative mood, you might turn to a longer paragraph because you wish to maintain continuity of thought without any break, and you can develop steady pace. There's no doubt you can create tension with a lengthy paragraph, but it's not the explosive, sudden variety; it's the building type of tension that must grow with the speed of your narrative ... slowly ... slowly burgeoning gradually ...

Not suddenly!
Like this!
Wham!

You can develop sudden tension by shortening paragraphs, by making them into one-sentence paragraphs, even one-word or one-syllable paragraphs:

He watched the door open.
It creaked.
No, it squealed.
And he remembered the morning of his mother's funeral.
Cold ...

The tension begins to turn to fright here, and the atmosphere is carried along by the abruptness of the style as much as by the actual words that are used. Not only do you hold the reader's attention, but you force the reader to zip down the page to stay with the action. The quick paragraph-cuts charge the atmosphere by speeding everything along, and tension is the result.

Then, when you want to calm things down, extend the paragraphs and sentences so they are longer and less abrupt. Stay with familiar words and phrases, mold your prose into a more congenial frame, and you'll come away with the conviction that grammar technique does indeed influence style.

As well as mood and atmosphere.

28

Don't Underestimate the Richness of the English Language

Ask a Frenchman, a German, a Scandinavian whether he had trouble learning English, and the answer will probably be: "Your language is difficult; it is not like one of our European tongues …"

Yet our country—and our language—sprung from a European base; once, hundreds of years ago, most of us *were* Europeans.

We are a polyglot nation, an amalgam of cultures, and our language reflects that. It's true that our language is also the language of the people inhabiting a group of islands near the French coast, but somehow they approach it differently than we do, and over the generations the differences have widened until it seems sometimes as if what *they* speak is not what *we* speak.

But skim the page of a major dictionary—any page will do. Note the word roots, often in italics, usually following the word itself and before the meaning or connotation. What impresses is the *variety* of places our language came from, the different cultures and civilizations that gave us the words we use. On a single page in my admittedly large dictionary, under H and stretching from "hue" to "hug" I found the following word-root designations: ME, OF, F, ML, Sc, MHG, G, Gr, Prov Eng … they stand for Middle (Medieval) English, Old French, French, Middle (Medieval) Latin, Scottish, Middle High German, German, Greek, Provincial English.

Is it any wonder that a Frenchman or a Dane or a Spaniard might have trouble with our language? We have taken from

so many sources, and we have fashioned a language that is a mosaic of expressions and understandings from other cultures and civilizations. In the diversity of our language roots lies the foundation for the richness of the way we communicate, and the results are vivid:

- —half the world's books are written in English
- —the majority of international telephone calls are made in English
- —60 percent of the world's radio programs are in English
- —70 percent of the world's mail is written and addressed in English
- —80 percent of the world's computer text is stored in English

One strong reason why all of this has happened is because our language is less mannered, less rigid than some others. The subtleties of meaning, the shades of effect in our words and phrases, allow more flexibility, and to anyone in the business of creating and communicating the written word, this is crucial.

Especially so when it comes to grammar. Rigid rules concerning adjectival endings, for example, don't exist in English. When we write about a white dove, we don't try to reconcile noun and adjective endings. But in Spanish or French or German this would have to be done. In Spanish, it's *la paloma blanca*, where the adjective must have a feminine ending to agree with the gender of the noun, which also is feminine. Something like that doesn't bother us. Our language is flexible enough to cover all contingencies, and our grammar takes it into account.

On the other hand, the very richness of our language can also complicate the interaction between our nouns and verbs. A single noun, for example, might offer several meanings, depending upon the verb with which it's used, and because of the polyglot foundations in our language the different verbs could come from different sources. Take the noun "bed":

Mother *made* the bed ... (Middle English)

The gardener *fertilized* the bed ... (Middle French)

The asphalt contractor *prepared* the roadbed ... (Latin)

If our grammar had been rigid, it is doubtful more than one verb could have worked with "bed," and it's equally doubtful "bed" could have several shades of meaning. But with our rich language, we don't have to worry about this, and it has its direct effect on our grammar. If our language is rich and flexible, then our grammar must be, also, and this means you should carry an appreciation for how our grammar influences the way we communicate. It doesn't do much good to maintain a rigid grammar outlook in the face of so many shades and subtleties of word meanings, and you should be prepared to change your grammar approach depending upon the prose you are working with.

There are more than two million words in the English language, and the list is open-ended. More words and phrases, and different meanings to established words and phrases, are attaching to our language every day, and grammatical effect must keep up. I recall an editor who caused me grief about this even though he should have known better. He contacted me to do a piece about the reenactment of a historical event. I had met him only once, and I had found him uninspiring (boring, actually) — but I am usually wary of first impressions of editors, so I put all of that aside and had no trouble working up enthusiasm for the piece.

The writing in his magazine was lively, so I decided to write a nonfiction piece long on dialogue and drama with italics and ellipses and the occasional capitalized phrase. It would be a *story*, not a dry narrative, and I knew that only a traditionalist would have trouble with it.

"Any problem with the piece?" I asked, after turning it in.

"Fine, fine," he responded.

I should have realized all was not fine when I received no

galleys or other communication from him. Then, one day I got a check and several copies of the magazine containing my article.

My anticipation turned to dismay when I saw what he had done. I had led the piece with an anecdote, but he had removed it completely, inserting, instead, a dry narrative about the historical significance of the story. He had removed every morsel of drama. What started out as a story had become a dry lecture. He had done away with my drama-inspired portrayal (including back and forth quotes and short, snappy paragraphs) and had fallen back on lengthy narrative, which also included lengthy paragraphs. It wasn't bad, I suppose, but it was dull, and that was exactly what I had been trying to avoid. The only item he didn't mangle was my use of italics, which I employed not for emphasis but for change of pace. He retained them, but he broadened them into whole paragraphs instead of pinpointing their use with individual words or phrases. He overkilled when he should not have gone hunting at all.

The richness of our language and the challenge that places on our grammar usage can be appreciated through the language gymnastics of Richard Lederer, who tells us in his essay, *The Strange Case of the English Language*:

> When we take the time to explore the paradoxes and vagaries of English, we find that hot dogs can be cold, darkrooms can be lit, homework can be done at school, nightmares can take place in broad daylight, while morning sickness and day dreaming can take place at night ...

Think of the delicate shades of meaning that produce such strange word usages; grammar and syntax must not be allowed to slide. You can't mix inappropriate active and passive verbs, for example, and then expect the word meanings to survive intact:

> He dialed the number, but the ringing wasn't there and the phone was hung up by someone ...

It doesn't read smoothly, and it's unclear whether the caller's or the callee's phone broke the connection. If the sentence stayed with active or passive voice throughout, we'd know, and we'd have no doubt who was doing what to whom. The richness of the grammar must match the richness of the prose.

At the same time, you can't be confined by the literalness of the words you use. Sometimes what you say makes no sense—if you take the words literally. Richard Lederer offers a few examples:

—a nonstop flight (this one never comes down)
—a near miss (isn't a miss, a miss?)
—watch your head (a hard thing to do with only one pair of eyes)

So we shade these meanings in order to give them realistic significance, and I've shown how expandable our language can be. It works the same way with grammar. The rule that says, "objects in a series shall be separated by commas" is fine until you wish to establish an emotional upgrade …*she saw redblueorangegreenflashes* … and so you expand your grammar usage by not following all the rules. Rich language should mean rich grammar.

Because the richer our language, the more opportunity there will be for grammar to shine and grow. The old rules work, but they do need polishing from time to time, and the savvy writer is always ready with the proper cloth.

29

DON'T BE AFRAID TO MAKE YOUR OWN RULES

There's an aphorism that seems appropriate for this, our final slice of grammar and style. A man is teaching his son to play golf, and he explains patiently that the stance should be as wide as the shoulders, that the ball should be placed two inches inside the left heel, that the head should remain still and the eyes should remain steadfast on the ball. "Oh," the father adds, "you should keep your weight evenly distributed, too."

The son frowns. "Why can't I swing my own way?"

"I'm trying to show you the *right* way."

"Why do I have to learn all these rules?"

The father laughs. "So you'll know which ones to break."

I had a publisher who put it a little differently but to the same effect. He was talking about his ledgers, which he alone maintained. Two other editors and a secretary/receptionist were also part of the office. I asked him why he didn't let one of them relieve him of the bookkeeping chores, and his answer was as concise as it was illuminating.

"They don't know which bills *not* to pay," he said.

All writers need to think this way to some extent (let me hasten to say I'm not advocating deadbeatism). I mean you have to be flexible when it comes to rules. You can't allow yourself to be so controlled that you shiver and shake when the urge to break them comes. Obviously, you need to know the rules *first*, but that's only preliminary; the real test is when to follow the rules and when to break them.

There's a writer's mindset we must all attain—there is no rule, *no rule* that can't be broken or changed! Nothing is everlasting.

And that goes for grammar and its rules, too. All through this book we've rattled old myths and flailed at timid thinking. Writers live and die by their imaginations, and the unforgiving enemy of imagination is the straightjacket of rules. You must be prepared to turn your back on rules—grammar rules in this context—if you hope to produce writing that attracts attention.

In simplest terms ... whatever works, works! And it doesn't matter what your eighth-grade teacher said. For example, suppose a single word is repeated *thirty* times in a row before a verb appears, and then after a second verb, the single word is repeated seven more times. Grammar purists would be highly offended because the sentence seems so out of balance. Yet that's exactly what Tom Wolfe did in a piece about Las Vegas and its gambling ambience. Here's the way he opened:

Hernia, hernia, hernia, hernia ... HERNIA ...

The word is repeated thirty times, without the capitalization and then he continued:

eight is the point, eight is the point, hernia, HERNia, hernia ...

It seems like a lot of nonsense, but a few paragraphs later he explains that craps dealers in Las Vegas keep up a running singsong and that it sounds like "... hernia, hernia, hernia ..."

Sometimes, of course, it doesn't work; be careful not to assume you can succeed every time out. *But keep trying!* The first thing you have to understand is that there's logic in the way grammar works, and such logic usually backs up the rules. There's a reason for periods or for paragraphs or for style consistency ... readers don't want to be confused, and you don't want to confuse them.

So, periods end sentences (which is like exhaling to end a breath), paragraphs offer the beginning and end of a thought or

spoken statement, and style consistency provides uniformity that maintains flow.

But as a writer you know there are times when the usual order and logic aren't so appealing, when you seek order and logic of a different sort, a fresh approach. When you want to make your own grammar rules and still avoid confusing the reader.

You can lower your margin for error by noting some things that probably won't work: a narrator, for example, who is barely literate and violates most standard grammar rules concerning verb objects, personal pronouns, parallelism and tenses. It's one thing if a minor character does these things, but when it's the narrator, the conduit through whom the reader gets into the story, it's both insulting and unattractive. Writers should have more respect for readers than to expect them to wade through verbal garbage.

Another grammar deviation that probably won't work is to ape the biblical style (with its begats and thees and thous) and apply it to a modern circumstance. It's like putting a wooden running board on a sleek sports car. In *The Psychiatric Fix*, my co-author and I wanted to portray the practice of psychiatry more as a religion than science and its practitioners more priest-like than health-concerned. So we opened the first chapter this way:

> In the beginning was The Word and The Word was Insanity. All who observed its affliction knew it and were afraid. Those who were afflicted were sinned against.
>
> And Insanity was The Word. It was the curse of a vengeful God...

It didn't work because it was inappropriate and snide. If psychiatry were a religion, we should have said so. Trying to become "biblical" only insulted people and turned them off. There was too great a gulf between the style and grammar techniques and the point we were trying to make.

No one has an infallible barometer on what will work, but other writers can be a source of aid. There isn't a writer walking

this earth who hasn't stretched to seek a fresh approach to grammar and style, and there isn't a writer who hasn't overreached. We have all experienced it, and sometimes it takes another (usually an editor) to tell us that what we're doing simply doesn't work. Writers can—and should—tell one another their experiences on what does and doesn't work, and in this give-and-take we can pare our errors.

The rules you make for yourself don't have to be elaborately different, but they do have to avoid distracting the reader from the basic story (one of the problems with our biblical rendering about psychiatry). A good maxim is to make grammar changes small at first, on the theory that the reader will be able to follow the story more easily (an occasional run-on sentence, for example), and then, if the story remains in control, other, more substantial, grammar changes can be made (entire paragraphs without verbs, strange indentations or mixing in whole sentences, even paragraphs, from another language).

The point is to make new grammar rules without distracting the reader. See how Karen Riles does it with her short story "Defection" which appeared in *The Southern Review*. The narrator has a new baby and lives along a creek. She doesn't like her new neighbors who always give gratuitous advice on how to manage her husband, do the lawn, raise her baby. The story, itself, contains no quotation marks, yet there is dialogue and interaction between the narrator and her neighbors. The author does it with italics:

> *Shade the seedlings from the midday sun*, they hollered, shrugging to each other in case I decided to discard the advice. *Use brown paper bags. If you water, do it after sunset. Put a hat on the baby...*

A half dozen times during the story she has the neighbors saying something, and each time the dialogue is designated by italics only. Otherwise, the entire story is unbroken narrative even to the climax, which includes a life-threatening event.

Does it work? Yes, it works well.

Why does it work? Because the author hasn't made a great leap in grammar technique. But she has made her own rule. If you examine the purpose behind quotation marks, you'll see they are used to distinguish them from narrative and to set off the fact that someone is speaking. In any scene, dialogue and narrative must work together, but they are different forms of expression, and they should not be scrambled together. Narrative is written one way, dialogue another way.

And Karen Riles has not tampered with these principles. *All she has done is italicize quotes instead of putting quotation marks around them.* The italicized portions stand out from the narrative just as if they had quotation marks, and they accomplish the same purpose.

Yet she has made her own rule, and she has been judicious about it. If her story had many more dialogue passages, would the technique of italics have worked as well? Probably not, because too many italics have the effect of reducing the significance of what is highlighted. In this sense, italics are like quotation marks, which are the universal symbol for dialogue. Since the use of italics is a deviation from the usual, she was careful about employing them only a half dozen times, and thus they stand out as if they were quotation marks.

And so a principle about making your own rules ... the larger the change to be made, the more difficult it will be to make that change work. Think purpose and effect—why do we want to make the change and does it accomplish the same thing as the grammar technique it replaces? If you're comfortable here, then you can fall back on your writing instincts and develop the new grammar rule. But if you have doubts, these will be reflected in your approach and subsequent style. You'll be tentative and inconsistent, a writer giving with the right hand and taking back with the left.

Readers know what to do with a writer like this because the writer's uncertainty will make the reader uncomfortable.

Slam! The book gets closed.

But if your confidence is bursting and you are sure your new approach will work, then go for it. Never, ever, assume that you must march to the same beat as everyone else.

Think bravely!

Act honestly!

Write imaginatively!

And make your own rules.

INDEX